The Folger Library General Reader's Shakespeare

THE TRAGEDY OF

ROMEO

and

JULIET

WILLIAM SHAKESPEARE

WSP

WASHINGTON SQUARE PRESS
PUBLISHED BY POCKET BOOKS
New York   London   Toronto   Sydney   Tokyo   Singapore

A Washington Square Press Publication of
POCKET BOOKS, a division of Simon & Schuster Inc.
1230 Avenue of the Americas, New York, NY 10020

ISBN: 0-671-72768-0

First Pocket Books printing December 1959

48 47 46 45 44 43

Preface

This edition of *Romeo and Juliet* is designed to make available a readable text of one of Shakespeare's most popular plays. In the centuries since Shakespeare many changes have occurred in the meanings of words, and some clarification of Shakespeare's vocabulary may be helpful. To provide the reader with necessary notes in the most accessible format, we have placed them on the pages facing the text that they explain. We have tried to make these notes as brief and simple as possible. Preliminary to the text we have also included a brief statement of essential information about Shakespeare and his stage. Readers desiring more detailed information should refer to the books suggested in the references, and if still further information is needed, the bibliographies in those books will provide the necessary clues to the literature of the subject.

The early texts of all of Shakespeare's plays provide only inadequate stage directions, and it is conventional for modern editors to add many that clarify the action. Such additions, and additions to entrances, are placed in square brackets.

All illustrations are from material in the Folger Library collections.

L. B. W.
V. A. L.

March 30, 1959

A Tragedy of Youthful Love

Romeo and Juliet is a young man's play, probably composed when Shakespeare was just at the turn of thirty, for the best evidence points to about 1595 as the date of its first appearance. It is written with the lyrical fervor of one who himself has experienced the passion of youthful love, but we have no knowledge of any event in Shakespeare's own life that focused his creative genius upon the theme of this play. In a dramatist as objective as Shakespeare, it is always dangerous to try to read into the author's lines evidence of his personal experience. But whatever the motivation, Shakespeare wrote a play that took its place almost at once in the immortal literature of love, a play that young men and women have cherished from that day to this as the ultimate glorification of ideal love.

When the play opens, Romeo is pining over a certain Rosaline, a coldhearted beauty unmoved by his protestations. Merely to get another glimpse of her, he and his fellows, Benvolio and Mercutio, crash the Capulets' party. While Romeo stands in a corner watching for Rosaline, Juliet dances by. From this point onward Romeo never has another thought of Rosaline; henceforth his affection centers upon Juliet with that singleness of devotion that romantics, especially in English-speaking countries, hold up as the ideal of true love. Juliet is that

Beauty too rich for use, for earth too dear!
So shows a snowy dove trooping with crows
As yonder lady o'er her fellows shows.

. . . .

Did my heart love till now? Forswear it, sight!
For I ne'er saw true beauty till this night.

Juliet is his great and final passion and there can never be another. For her he will venture even life itself, and life without her will be merely a worthless bauble. This idea of an overwhelming passion that comes to true lovers once in a lifetime is a common motif in English poetry and fiction, and young people find it easy to subscribe to such a doctrine of unalterable love. Only the aged and the cynical would suggest that Romeo might easily find another Juliet tomorrow.

The love that Romeo and Juliet display is of the idealistic type that comes sometimes with the suddenness and the devastating effect of a stroke of lightning. Once having been touched by such a passion, no man or maid is ever the same again. He or she becomes a dedicated soul, dedicated to union with the one and only object of this transmuting affection. The force of an overwhelming love that purifies and matures the protagonists is the dominant theme of *Romeo and Juliet*, and for more than three and a half centuries sentiments in this play have exerted a romantic influence upon countless readers. The probability is that it has subtly affected the attitude of the English-speaking peoples toward love. The extent of this influence one can only conjecture, but generations of young people have felt a deep emotional response to the play. It has been a part of nearly every literate person's emotional experience. At some point in his youth, nearly every man has idealized a Juliet no whit less glorious than the heroine of the play. Doubtless every girl has also seen herself as the object of such transcendent affection as Romeo's. And thereby perhaps has come much grief. But the realities that maturity brings never spoil the play even for the coldest septuagenarian, who may look back upon the poetry in this drama with a tender glow of remembered youth.

Romeo and Juliet is not one of Shakespeare's cosmic tragedies like *King Lear*, *Othello*, or *Hamlet*. In the Greek concept of the tragic hero as a great personage destroyed by some tragic flaw, Romeo has no place. Romeo is merely a young man in love with love and it is his misfortune that at a critical moment in his emotional development his eye falls upon the beautiful daughter of his father's enemy. The disasters that befall the protagonists all flow from this situation. The play is a drama of pathos and pity rather than the type of soul-purging tragedy that Shakespeare wrote in his maturity. The author himself is fully conscious of the kind of play that he has composed and in the prologue he makes clear to the spectators what they are to see enacted:

> From forth the fatal loins of these two foes
> A pair of star-crossed lovers take their life,
> Whose misadventured piteous overthrows
> Doth with their death bury their parents' strife.

The Fates are perverse and these lovers are the victims of some ill conjunction of the stars from which there is no escape. A cruel destiny sweeps them to their unhappy ends while the spectators look on with pity and sadness.

One need not search this play for profound moral lessons. Shakespeare was not writing a sermon or providing instruction for young people. He was placing upon the stage a romantic story, not unknown to literary folk, and he concentrated upon those elements of character and situation best suited to dramatic interpretation. When Shakespeare wrote *Romeo and Juliet* he was not a beginner, for he had already had a part in writing *Henry VI*, and had completed *Richard III*, *The Comedy of Errors*, *Titus Andronicus*, *The Taming of the Shrew*, *The Two Gentlemen of Verona*, and *Love's Labour's Lost*; but only in *Richard III* and in the terrible *Titus Andronicus* had he tried his hand at tragic drama. He had not yet acquired the philosophic depth revealed in his more mature plays, and he was still experimenting with characterization and its dramatic portrayal.

Though *Romeo and Juliet* comes relatively early in Shakespeare's career as a playwright, it reveals a sureness of touch that shows how successfully he had mastered the techniques of his theatre. Vivid poetry is wedded to brilliant characterization and the action is rapid and tense. To give light and shade to the portrayal of the principal characters Shakespeare includes minor figures whose words and actions supply contrast and color. Although he centers our interest upon the idealistic love of Romeo and Juliet, he provides contrasts in the characterizations of the ribald Mercutio the materialistic ambitions of the matchmaking Capulets, and the Nurse's recollections of sensual pleasures The comic parts are not overplayed and are just sufficient to give relief from tragic action that otherwise would keep the play at too high a tension.

Romeo and Juliet has a whole gallery of characters who are drawn with fidelity to life. For example, old Capulet is a busy, bustling master of the house who must see to every detail and have a hand in all the preparations for the wedding Mercutio is a dashing fellow whose role is frequently preferred by actors to the part of Romeo.

Friar Laurence is clearly drawn as a devout, well-meaning spiritual guide who, with the best of intentions, tries to help and unwittingly becomes the instrument of disaster. Even the servants have realistic parts. This attention to minor characters helps to explain why *Romeo and Juliet* has been a favorite with the players. There are other meaty roles in addition to the leads.

Romeo and Juliet is notable for its lyrical qualities. At times the lyrical poet runs away with the play and inserts lines of sheer poetic exuberance. Mercutio's speech on Queen Mab (I. [iv.] 57 ff.) is a passage that reads as if it had fallen out of *A Midsummer Night's Dream* by mistake. Shakespeare the poet goes off in a flight of fancy and takes delight in imagery, metaphor, and the evocation of a fairy world that a little later was to produce Titania and Oberon. Elsewhere throughout the play he provides a light touch of lyrical expression and creates lines that have become a part of our heritage of quotations. Occasionally, however, the author drops into the rhetorical patter of wordplay beloved of the Elizabethans but now out of fashion, as in the passage ([III. ii.] 48 ff.) in which Juliet plays on the pronoun "I":

> Hath Romeo slain himself? Say thou but "I,"
> And that bare vowel "I" shall poison more
> Than the death-darting eye of cockatrice.
> I am not I, if there be such an "I";
> Or those eyes shut that make thee answer "I."
> If he be slain, say "I"; or if not, "no."

The Elizabethans generally found pleasure in the use of words and in rhetorical tricks. In *Romeo and Juliet,* Shakespeare follows the fashion in rhetorical devices, but in the finest passages the poet transcends the rhetorician.

Emotion rises to a pitch of intensity and even conventional poetic expressions acquire life and vividness, as for example in Juliet's complaint at the Nurse's slowness ([II. v.] 4 ff.):

> O, she is lame! Love's heralds should be thoughts,
> Which ten times faster glide than the sun's beams
> Driving back shadows over lowering hills.
> Therefore do nimble-pinioned doves draw Love,
> And therefore hath the wind-swift Cupid wings.

In passages of great emotional tension, the language becomes simple and direct. At the moment of parting, Romeo tries to pretend that day is not breaking in the East and Juliet replies ([III. v.] 26 ff.):

> It is, it is! Hie hence, be gone, away!
> It is the lark that sings so out of tune,
> Straining harsh discords and unpleasing sharps.
> Some say the lark makes sweet division;
> This doth not so, for she divideth us.
> Some say the lark and loathed toad changed eyes;
> O, now I would they had changed voices too,
> Since arm from arm that voice doth us affray,
> Hunting thee hence with hunt's-up to the day!
> O, now be gone! More light and light it grows.

Although the poet is still using conventional imagery, the words are short and plain and the meaning is sincere and intense. *Romeo and Juliet* demonstrates Shakespeare's growing power as a lyrical poet.

Shakespeare achieved a new success in *Romeo and Juliet*, which was immediately popular on its first appearance; from that day to this it has been seen constantly in the theatre, though not always in the precise form in which Shakespeare wrote it. Its early popularity was such that a printed version appeared in 1597, the title page stating that it had "been often (with great applause) plaid publiquely." Between the appearance of this First Quarto and the publication of the First Folio edition of the plays in 1623, three other quarto versions found their way into print, and a Fifth Quarto edition appeared in 1637. These numerous printings testify to the desire of the public for reading versions of a play that had made an extraordinary impression on the stage.

The playhouses were closed from 1642 to 1660 during the Puritan Revolution, but when they reopened, at the Restoration of Charles II, *Romeo and Juliet* was one of the plays of Shakespeare selected for revival, and it regained at once its place on the popular stage. Someone prepared an edition with a happy ending in which hero and heroine were saved and lived happily ever after. Two versions, one tragic and one happy, played on alternate nights and spectators could choose whichever suited their mood.

The early eighteenth century saw various adaptations of the play, including an imitation by Thomas Otway and another by Theophilus Cibber. In 1748, David Garrick staged an adaptation of his own at Drury Lane, while at nearby Covent Garden still another version was running at the same time. The rivalry of the actors and actresses was keen, and players and audiences took sides in a partisan war of the theatres over the play. Operatic versions of *Romeo and Juliet* reduced the play to musical spectacle and enjoyed a momentary popularity.

In the early nineteenth century, a revival of *Romeo and Juliet* in which Fanny Kemble played Juliet was such a success that it saved Covent Garden Theatre from one of its periodic financial crises. Throughout the nineteenth century the play remained almost constantly on the stage, both in England and America. Sometimes the version was an adaptation; at other times the play was acted much as Shakespeare had written it. Most of the great actors and actresses of the nineteenth and twentieth centuries have at some time in their careers acted in this play. Several motion picture versions have had brief successes.

On the continent of Europe it was a success from the first and, indeed, a French play on the subject of Romeo and Juliet preceded Shakespeare's play by fourteen years, but there is no evidence that Shakespeare knew the French drama. A Dutch play on the Romeo and Juliet story and German versions date from the early seventeenth century. A version of Shakespeare's play was acted in Germany and adaptations from it were made in German. In later periods Shakespeare's *Romeo and Juliet* has been almost as popular abroad as it has been in England. In Verona enterprising folk have made a tourists' attraction of a building known as "Juliet's house" and one can visit another attraction called "Romeo and Juliet's grave."

SOURCES OF THE PLAY

As in many other Elizabethan plays, the plot of *Romeo and Juliet* goes back to an Italian short story. Incidents, situations, and characters vaguely similar to those found in the play occur in several tales preserved in col-

AN
EXCELLENT
conceited Tragedie
OF
Romeo and Iuliet.

As it hath been often (with great applause)
plaid publiquely, by the right Ho-
nourable the L. of *Hunsdon*
his Seruants.

LONDON,
Printed by Iohn Danter.
1597

The title page of the First Quarto of *Romeo and Juliet*.

lections of Renaissance Italian stories. The story in one version was given an historical setting in Verona about 1303, during the rule of Bartolomeo della Scala, the Prince Escalus of Shakespeare's play. Matteo Bandello, in 1554, included a Romeo and Juliet story in his *Novelle* and this was translated into French by Pierre Boaistuau and appears in the *Histoires Tragiques* (1559). From the French, William Painter translated the tale into English and included it in his collection entitled *The Palace of Pleasure* (1565-67). From Boaistuau, Arthur Brooke also presumably took the material which he wove into a long narrative poem called *The Tragical History of Romeus and Juliet* (1562).

Although Shakespeare appears to have read Painter's story, and perhaps other versions, he followed Brooke's poem closely and made it his immediate and principal source Brooke's statement that he had seen on the stage a play on the subject has led some scholars to believe that Shakespeare reworked an old play; but if he did, we know nothing of it. Shakespeare based his play in most essential points on Brooke's poem.

THE TEXTUAL PROBLEM

The text of *Romeo and Juliet* presents complicated problems that offer no easy solution. The First Quarto version of 1597 is classified as a "Bad Quarto." That is, it seems to have been a pirated version, "reported" by one or more actors who remembered parts and reproduced the lines from memory as best they could. Garbled and curtailed as some of the passages are, Quarto I has many readings that are better than those that appear in later texts. For those interested, we have appended a list at the back of this volume tabulating the instances where the First

Quarto reading has appeared preferable to us. This Quarto also contains a number of detailed stage directions not found in later editions; many of these we have included because of the light they throw on the staging of the play in Shakespeare's own lifetime.

The Second Quarto of 1599, "Newly corrected, augmented, and amended," is supposed to have been printed from a playhouse copy, and one would assume that it represents the authorized version insofar as there is one that had the sanction of Shakespeare's company. As has been the general editorial practice, we have used the Second Quarto as the basis of our text, but we have accepted readings from the First Quarto, the Folio, and occasionally from the other early Quartos when they seemed to correct obviously bad readings. For the truth is that the Second Quarto is also sometimes garbled and sometimes gives poor readings. The use by the printer of a playhouse text is no guarantee of legible copy, and that it was the legitimate acting version is no assurance that it represents the authentic words that Shakespeare wrote. Anyone familiar with the practices of actors and producers, Elizabethan or modern, knows that acting copy is often altered and scribbled over The sorry state of the playhouse copy, even if originally written in Shakespeare's fairest hand, may account for the many errors in the Second Quarto.

A Third Quarto of 1609 was printed from the Second Quarto; the Folio version of 1623 and an undated Fourth Quarto follow the text of the Third Quarto. Yet all of these introduce some independent and occasionally improved readings The best that a modern editor can do is to collate the early versions and choose the readings that best represent the meaning that was apparently intended. The analysis of the texts by the most skillful students of bibliographical science cannot insure that a reading is

Shakespeare's own or that it does not represent some tinkering in the playhouse. No sanctity of Holy Writ attaches to Shakespeare's or to any other dramatic text in the Elizabethan period.

THE AUTHOR

As early as 1598 Shakespeare was so well known as a literary and dramatic craftsman that Francis Meres, in his *Palladis Tamia: Wits Treasury,* referred in flattering terms to him as "mellifluous and honey-tongued Shakespeare," famous for his *Venus and Adonis,* his *Lucrece,* and "his sugared sonnets," which were circulating "among his private friends." Meres observes further that "as Plautus and Seneca are accounted the best for comedy and tragedy among the Latins, so Shakespeare among the English is the most excellent in both kinds for the stage," and he mentions a dozen plays that had made a name for Shakespeare. He concludes with the remark "that the Muses would speak with Shakespeare's fine filed phrase if they would speak English."

To those acquainted with the history of the Elizabethan and Jacobean periods, it is incredible that anyone should be so naïve or ignorant as to doubt the reality of Shakespeare as the author of the plays that bear his name. Yet so much nonsense has been written about other "candidates" for the plays that it is well to remind readers that no credible evidence that would stand up in a court of law has ever been adduced to prove either that Shakespeare did not write his plays or that anyone else wrote them. All the theories offered for the authorship of Francis Bacon, the Earl of Derby, the Earl of Oxford, the Earl of Hertford, Christopher Marlowe, and a score of other candidates are mere conjectures spun from the active imaginations of persons who confuse hypothesis and conjecture with evidence.

As Meres' statement of 1598 indicates, Shakespeare was already a popular playwright whose name carried weight at the box office. The obvious reputation of Shakespeare as early as 1598 makes the effort to prove him a myth one of the most absurd in the history of human perversity.

The anti-Shakespeareans talk darkly about a plot of vested interests to maintain the authorship of Shakespeare. Nobody has any vested interest in Shakespeare, but every scholar is interested in the truth and in the quality of evidence advanced by special pleaders who set forth hypotheses in place of facts.

The anti-Shakespeareans base their arguments upon a few simple premises, all of them false. These false premises are that Shakespeare was an unlettered yokel without any schooling, that nothing is known about Shakespeare, and that only a noble lord or the equivalent in background could have written the plays. The facts are that more is known about Shakespeare than about most dramatists of his day, that he had a very good education, acquired in the Stratford Grammar School, that the plays show no evidence of profound book learning, and that the knowledge of kings and courts evident in the plays is no greater than any intelligent young man could have picked up at second hand. Most anti-Shakespeareans are naïve and betray an obvious snobbery. The author of their favorite plays, they imply, must have had a college diploma framed and hung on his study wall like the one in their dentist's office, and obviously so great a writer must have had a title or some equally significant evidence of exalted social background. They forget that genius has a way of cropping up in unexpected places and that none of the great creative writers of the world got his inspiration in a college or university course.

William Shakespeare was the son of John Shakespeare of Stratford-upon-Avon, a substantial citizen of that small but busy market town in the center of the rich agricultural county of Warwick. John Shakespeare kept a shop, what we would call a general store; he dealt in wool and other produce and gradually acquired property. As a youth, John Shakespeare had learned the trade of glover and leather worker. There is no contemporary evidence that the elder Shakespeare was a butcher, though the anti-Shakespeareans like to talk about the ignorant "butcher's boy of Stratford." Their only evidence is a statement by gossipy John Aubrey, more than a century after William Shakespeare's birth, that young William followed his father's trade, and when he killed a calf, "he would do it in a high style and make a speech." We would like to believe the story true, but Aubrey is not a very credible witness.

John Shakespeare probably continued to operate a farm at Snitterfield that his father had leased. He married Mary Arden, daughter of his father's landlord, a man of some property. The third of their eight children was William, baptized on April 26, 1564, and probably born three days before. At least, it is conventional to celebrate April 23 as his birthday.

The Stratford records give considerable information about John Shakespeare. We know that he held several municipal offices including those of alderman and mayor. In 1580 he was in some sort of legal difficulty and was fined for neglecting a summons of the Court of Queen's Bench requiring him to appear at Westminster and be bound over to keep the peace.

As a citizen and alderman of Stratford, John Shakespeare was entitled to send his son to the grammar school free. Though the records are lost, there can be no reason to doubt that this is where young William received his education. As any student of the period knows, the grammar schools provided the basic education in Latin learning and literature. The Elizabethan grammar school is not to be confused with modern grammar schools. Many cultivated men of the day received all their formal education in the grammar schools. At the universities in this period a student would have received little training that would have inspired him to be a creative writer. At Stratford young Shakespeare would have acquired a familiarity with Latin and some little knowledge of Greek. He would have read Latin authors and become acquainted with the plays of Plautus and Terence. Undoubtedly, in this period of his life he received that stimulation to read and explore for himself the world of ancient and modern history which he later utilized in his plays. The youngster who does not acquire this type of intellectual curiosity *before* college days rarely develops as a result of a college course the kind of mind Shakespeare demonstrated. His learning in books was anything but profound, but he clearly had the probing curiosity that sent him in search of information, and he had a keenness in the observation of nature and of humankind that finds reflection in his poetry.

There is little documentation for Shakespeare's boyhood. There is little reason why there should be. Nobody knew that he was going to be a dramatist about whom any scrap of information would be prized in the centuries to come. He was merely an active and vigorous youth of Stratford, perhaps assisting his father in his business, and no Boswell bothered to write down facts about him. The most important record that we have is a marriage license issued by the Bishop of Worcester on November 28, 1582, to permit William Shakespeare to marry Anne Hathaway, seven or eight years his senior; furthermore, the Bishop permitted the marriage after reading the banns only once instead of three times, evidence of the desire for haste. The need was explained on May 26, 1583, when the christening of Susanna, daughter of William and Anne Shakespeare, was recorded at Stratford. Two years later, on February 2, 1585, the records show the birth of twins to the Shakespeares, a boy and a girl who were christened Hamnet and Judith.

What William Shakespeare was doing in Stratford during the early years of his married life, or when he went to London, we do not know. It has been conjectured that he tried his hand at schoolteaching, but that is a mere guess. There is a legend that he left Stratford to escape a charge of poaching in the park of Sir Thomas Lucy of Charlecote, but there is no proof of this. There is also a legend that when first he came to London, he earned his living by holding horses outside a playhouse and presently was given employment inside, but there is nothing better than eighteenth-century hearsay for this. How Shakespeare broke into the London theatres as a dramatist and actor we do not know. But lack of information is not surprising, for Elizabethans did not write their autobiographies, and we know even less about the lives of many writers and some men of affairs than we know about Shakespeare. By 1592 he was so well established and popular that he incurred the envy of the dramatist and pamphleteer Robert Greene, who referred to him as an "upstart crow . . . in his own conceit the only Shake-scene in a country." From this time onward, contemporary allusions and references in legal documents enable the scholar to chart Shakespeare's career with greater accuracy than is possible with most other Elizabethan dramatists.

By 1594 Shakespeare was a member of the company of actors known as the Lord Chamberlain's Men. After the accession of James I, in 1603, the company would have the sovereign for their patron and would be known as the King's Men During the period of its greatest prosperity, this company would have as its principal theatres the Globe and the Blackfriars Shakespeare was both an actor and a shareholder in the company. Tradition has assigned him such acting roles as Adam in *As You Like It* and the Ghost in *Hamlet*, a modest place on the stage that suggests that he may have had other duties in the management of the company. Such conclusions, however, are based on surmise.

What we do know is that his plays were popular and that he was highly successful in his vocation. His first play may have been *The Comedy of Errors*, acted perhaps in 1591. Certainly this was one of his earliest plays. The three parts of *Henry VI* were acted sometime between 1590 and 1592 Critics are not in agreement about precisely how much Shakespeare wrote of these three plays. *Richard III* probably dates from 1593 With this play Shakespeare captured the imagination of Elizabethan audiences then enormously interested in historical plays. With *Richard III* Shakespeare also gave an interpretation pleasing to the Tudors of the rise to power of the grandfather of Queen Elizabeth. From this time onward, Shakespeare's plays followed on the stage in rapid succession: *Titus Andronicus, The Taming of the Shrew, The Two Gentlemen of Verona, Love's Labour's Lost, Romeo and Juliet, Richard II, A Midsummer Night's Dream, King John, The Merchant of Venice, Henry IV*, Pts. I and II, *Much Ado About Nothing, Henry V, Julius Cæsar, As You*

Like It, Twelfth Night, Hamlet, The Merry Wives of Windsor, All's Well That Ends Well, Measure for Measure, Othello, King Lear, and nine others that followed before Shakespeare retired completely, about 1613.

In the course of his career in London, he made enough money to enable him to retire to Stratford with a competence. His purchase on May 4, 1597, of New Place, then the second-largest dwelling in Stratford, a "pretty house of brick and timber," with a handsome garden, indicates his increasing prosperity. There his wife and children lived while he busied himself in the London theatres. The summer before he acquired New Place, his life was darkened by the death of his only son, Hamnet, a child of eleven. In May, 1602, Shakespeare purchased one hundred and seven acres of fertile farmland near Stratford and a few months later bought a cottage and garden across the alley from New Place. About 1611, he seems to have returned permanently to Stratford, for the next year a legal document refers to him as "William Shakespeare of Stratford-upon-Avon . . . gentleman." To achieve the desired appellation of gentleman, William Shakespeare had seen to it that the College of Heralds in 1596 granted his father a coat of arms. In one step he thus became a second-generation gentleman.

Shakespeare's daughter Susanna made a good match in 1607 with Dr. John Hall, a prominent and prosperous Stratford physician. His second daughter, Judith, did not marry until she was thirty-two years old, and then, under somewhat scandalous circumstances, she married Thomas Quiney, a Stratford vintner. On March 25, 1616, Shakespeare made his will, bequeathing his landed property to Susanna, £300 to Judith, certain sums to other relatives, and his second-best bed to his wife, Anne. Much has been made of the second-best bed, but the legacy probably indicates only that Anne liked that particular bed. Shakespeare, following the practice of the time, may have already arranged with Susanna for his wife's care. Finally, on April 23, 1616, the anniversary of his birth, William Shakespeare died, and he was buried on April 25 within the chancel of Trinity Church, as befitted an honored citizen. On August 6, 1623, a few months before the publication of the collected edition of Shakespeare's plays, Anne Shakespeare joined her husband in death.

THE PUBLICATION OF HIS PLAYS

During his lifetime Shakespeare made no effort to publish any of his plays, though eighteen appeared in print in single-play editions known as quartos. Some of these are corrupt versions known as "bad quartos." No quarto, so far as is known, had the author's approval. Plays were not considered "literature" any more than most radio and television scripts today are considered literature. Dramatists sold their plays outright to the theatrical companies and it was usually considered in the company's interest to keep plays from getting into print. To achieve a reputation as a man of letters, Shakespeare wrote his *Sonnets* and his narrative poems, *Venus and Adonis* and *The Rape of Lucrece*, but he probably never dreamed that his plays would establish his reputation as a literary genius. Only Ben Jonson, a man known for his colossal conceit, had the crust to call his plays *Works*, as he did when he published an edition in 1616. But men laughed at Ben Jonson.

After Shakespeare's death, two of his old colleagues in the King's Men, John Heminges and Henry Condell, decided that it would be a good thing to print, in more accurate versions than were then available, the plays already published and eighteen additional plays not previously published in quarto. In 1623 appeared *Mr. William Shake-speares Comedies, Histories, & Tragedies. Published according to the True Originall Copies. London. Printed by Isaac Iaggard and Ed. Blount* This was the famous First Folio, a work that had the authority of Shakespeare's associates. The only play commonly attributed to Shakespeare that was omitted in the First Folio was *Pericles.* In their preface, "To the great Variety of Readers," Heminges and Condell state that whereas "you were abused with diverse stolen and surreptitious copies, maimed and deformed by the frauds and stealths of injurious impostors that exposed them, even those are now offered to your view cured and perfect of their limbs; and all the rest, absolute in their numbers, as he conceived them." What they used for printer's copy is one of the vexed problems of scholarship, and skilled bibliographers have devoted years of study to the question of the relation of the "copy" for the First Folio to Shakespeare's manuscripts. In some cases it is clear that the editors corrected printed quarto versions of the plays, probably by comparison with playhouse scripts. Whether these scripts were in Shakespeare's autograph is anybody's guess. No manuscript of any play in Shakespeare's handwriting has survived. Indeed, very few play manuscripts from this period by any author are extant. The Tudor and Stuart periods had not yet learned to prize autographs and authors' original manuscripts.

Since the First Folio contains eighteen plays not previously printed, it is the only source for these. For the other eighteen, which had appeared in quarto versions, the First Folio also has the authority of an edition prepared and overseen by Shakespeare's colleagues and professional associates. But since editorial standards in 1623 were far from strict, and Heminges and Condell were actors rather than editors by profession, the texts are sometimes careless. The printing and proofreading of the First Folio also left much to be desired, and some garbled passages have to be corrected and emended. The "good quarto" texts have to be taken into account in preparing a modern edition.

Because of the great popularity of Shakespeare through the centuries, the First Folio has become a prized book, but it is not a very rare one, for it is estimated that 238 copies are extant. The Folger Shakespeare Library in Washington, D.C., has seventy-nine copies of the First Folio, collected by the founder, Henry Clay Folger, who believed that a collection of as many texts as possible would reveal significant facts about the text of Shakespeare's plays. Dr. Charlton Hinman, using an ingenious machine of his own invention for mechanical collating, has made many discoveries that throw light on Shakespeare's text and on printing practices of the day.

The probability is that the First Folio of 1623 had an edition of between 1,000 and 1,250 copies. It is believed that it sold for £1, which made it an expensive book, for £1 in 1623 was equivalent to something between $40 and $50 in modern purchasing power.

During the seventeenth century, Shakespeare was sufficiently popular to warrant three later editions in folio size, the Second Folio of 1632, the Third Folio of 1663-1664, and the Fourth Folio of 1685. The Third Folio added six other plays ascribed to Shakespeare, but these are apocryphal.

THE SHAKESPEAREAN THEATRE

The theatres in which Shakespeare's plays were performed were vastly different from those we know today. The stage was a platform that jutted out into the area now occupied by the first rows of seats on the main floor, what is called the "orchestra" in America and the "pit" in England. This platform had no curtain to come down at the ends of acts and scenes. And although simple stage properties were available, the Elizabethan theatre lacked both the machinery and the elaborate movable scenery of the modern theatre. In the rear of the platform stage was a curtained area that could be used as an inner room, a tomb, or any such scene that might be required. A balcony above this inner room, and perhaps balconies on the sides of the stage, could represent the upper deck of a ship, the entry to Juliet's room, or a prison window. A trap door in the stage provided an entrance for ghosts and devils from the nether regions, and a similar trap in the canopied structure over the stage, known as the "heavens," made it possible to let down angels on a rope. These primitive stage arrangements help to account for many elements in Elizabethan plays. For example, since there was no curtain, the dramatist frequently felt the necessity of writing into his play action to clear the stage at the ends of acts and scenes. The funeral march at the end of *Hamlet* is not there merely for atmosphere; Shakespeare had to get the corpses off the stage. The lack of scenery also freed the dramatist from undue concern about the exact location of his sets, and the physical relation of his various settings to each other did not have to be worked out with the same precision as in the modern theatre.

Before London had buildings designed exclusively for theatrical entertainment, plays were given in inns and taverns. The characteristic inn of the period had an inner courtyard with rooms opening onto balconies overlooking the yard. Players could set up their temporary stages at one end of the yard and audiences could find seats on the balconies out of the weather. The poorer sort could stand or sit on the cobblestones in the yard, which was open to the sky. The first theatres followed this construction, and throughout the Elizabethan period the large public theatres had a yard in front of the stage open to the weather, with two or three tiers of covered balconies extending around the theatre. This physical structure again influenced the writing of plays. Because a dramatist wanted the actors to be heard, he frequently wrote into his play orations that could be delivered with declamatory effect. He also provided spectacle, buffoonery, and broad jests to keep the riotous groundlings in the yard entertained and quiet.

In another respect the Elizabethan theatre differed greatly from ours. It had no actresses. All women's roles were taken by boys, sometimes recruited from the boys' choirs of the London churches. Some of these youths acted their roles with great skill and the Elizabethans did not seem to be aware of any incongruity. The first actresses on the professional English stage appeared after the Restoration of Charles II, in 1660, when exiled Englishmen brought back from France practices of the French stage.

London in the Elizabethan period, as now, was the center of theatrical interest, though wandering actors from time to time traveled through the country performing in inns, halls, and the houses of the nobility. The first professional playhouse, called simply The Theatre, was erected by James Burbage, father of Shakespeare's colleague Richard Burbage, in 1576 on lands of the old Holywell Priory adjacent to Finsbury Fields, a playground and park area just north of the city walls. It had the advantage of being outside the city's jurisdiction and yet was near enough to be easily accessible. Soon after The Theatre was opened, another playhouse called The

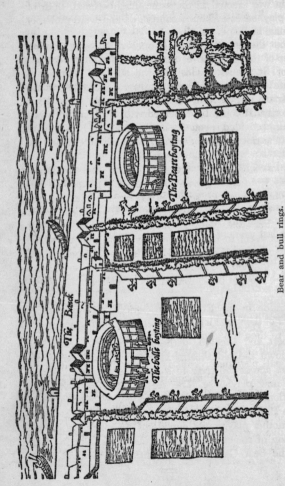

Bear and bull rings.

From Agas' Map of London (reproduced from J. Q. Adams, *Shakespearean Playhouses*).

Curtain was erected in the same neighborhood. Both of these playhouses had open courtyards and were probably polygonal in shape.

About the time The Curtain opened, Richard Farrant, Master of the Children of the Chapel Royal at Windsor and of St. Paul's, conceived the idea of opening a "private" theatre in the old monastery buildings of the Blackfriars, not far from St. Paul's Cathedral in the heart of the city. This theatre was ostensibly to train the choirboys in plays for presentation at Court, but Farrant managed to present plays to paying audiences and achieved considerable success until aristocratic neighbors complained and had the theatre closed. This first Blackfriars Theatre was significant, however, because it popularized the boy actors in a professional way and it paved the way for a second theatre in the Blackfriars, which Shakespeare's company took over more than thirty years later. By the last years of the sixteenth century, London had at least six professional theatres and still others were erected during the reign of James I.

The Globe Theatre, the playhouse that most people connect with Shakespeare, was erected early in 1599 on the Bankside, the area across the Thames from the city. Its construction had a dramatic beginning, for on the night of December 28, 1598, James Burbage's sons, Cuthbert and Richard, gathered together a crew who tore down the old theatre in Holywell and carted the timbers across the river to a site that they had chosen for a new playhouse. The reason for this clandestine operation was a row with the landowner over the lease to the Holywell property. The site chosen for the Globe was another playground outside of the city's jurisdiction, a region of somewhat unsavory character. Not far away was the Bear Garden, an amphitheatre devoted to the baiting of bears and bulls. This was also the region occupied by many houses of ill fame licensed by the Bishop of Winchester and the source of substantial revenue to him. But it was easily accessible either from London Bridge or by means of the cheap boats operated by the London watermen, and it had the great advantage of being beyond the authority of the Puritanical alderman of London, who frowned on plays because they lured apprentices from work, filled their heads with improper ideas, and generally exerted a bad influence. The aldermen also complained that the crowds drawn together in the theatre helped to spread the plague.

The Globe was the handsomest theatre up to its time. It was a large building, apparently octagonal in shape and open like its predecessors to the sky in the center, but capable of seating a large audience in its covered balconies. To erect and operate the Globe, the Burbages organized a syndicate composed of the leading members of the dramatic company, of which Shakespeare was a member. Since it was open to the weather and depended on natural light, plays had to be given in the afternoon. This caused no hardship in the long afternoons of an English summer, but in the winter the weather was a great handicap and discouraged all except the hardiest. For that reason, in 1608 Shakespeare's company was glad to take over the lease of the second Blackfriars Theatre, a substantial, roomy hall reconstructed within the framework of the old monastery building. This theatre was protected from the weather and its stage was artificially lighted by chandeliers of candles. This became the winter playhouse for Shakespeare's company and at once proved so popular that the congestion of traffic created an embarrassing problem. Stringent regulations had to be made for the movement of coaches in the vicinity. Shake-

The Globe

The Globe Playhouse.
From Visscher's *View of London* (1616).

speare's company continued to use the Globe during the summer months. In 1613 a squib fired from a cannon during a performance of *Henry VII* fell on the thatched roof and the Globe burned to the ground. The next year it was rebuilt.

London had other famous theatres. The Rose, just west of the Globe, was built by Philip Henslowe, a semiliterate denizen of the Bankside, who became one of the most important theatrical owners and producers of the Tudor and Stuart periods. What is more important for historians, he kept a detailed account book, which provides much of our information about theatrical history in his time. Another famous theatre on the Bankside was the Swan, which a Dutch priest Johannes de Witt visited in 1596. The crude drawing of the stage which he made was copied by his friend Arend van Buchell; it is one of the important pieces of contemporary evidence for theatrical construction. Among the other theatres, the Fortune, north of the city, on Golding Lane, and the Red Bull, even farther away from the city, off St. John's Street, were the most popular. The Red Bull, much frequented by apprentices, favored sensational and sometimes rowdy plays.

The actors who kept all of these theatres going were organized into companies under the protection of some noble patron. Traditionally actors had enjoyed a low reputation. In some of the ordinances they were classed as vagrants; in the phraseology of the time, "rogues, vagabonds, sturdy beggars, and common players" were all listed together as undesirables. To escape penalties often meted out to these characters, organized groups of actors managed to gain the protection of various personages of high degree. In the later years of Elizabeth's reign, a group flourished under the name of the Queen's Men;

tectum

Porticus

sedilia

orchestra

mimorum
ædes

ingressus

proscænium

planities siue arena.

quintum sed dispari et poculuirea, bestiarum conflictai
oni destinatum, in quo multi vrsi, tauri, et stupenda
magnitudinis canes, distinctis caueis et septis aluntur; qui
ad

Interior of the Swan Theatre.
From a drawing by Johannes de Witt (1596).

another group had the protection of the Lord Admiral and were known as the Lord Admiral's Men. Edward Alleyn, son-in-law of Philip Henslowe, was the leading spirit in the Lord Admiral's Men. Besides the adult companies, troupes of boy actors from time to time also enjoyed considerable popularity. Among these were the Children of Paul's and the Children of the Chapel Royal.

The company with which Shakespeare had a long association had for its first patron Henry Carey, Lord Hunsdon, the Lord Chamberlain, and hence they were known as the Lord Chamberlain's Men. After the accession of James I, they became the King's Men. This company was the great rival of the Lord Admiral's Men, managed by Henslowe and Alleyn.

All was not easy for the players in Shakespeare's time, for the aldermen of London were always eager for an excuse to close up the Blackfriars and any other theatres in their jurisdiction. The theatres outside the jurisdiction of London were not immune from interference, for they might be shut up by order of the Privy Council for meddling in politics or for various other offenses, or they might be closed in time of plague lest they spread infection. During plague times, the actors usually went on tour and played the provinces wherever they could find an audience. Particularly frightening were the plagues of 1592–1594 and 1613 when the theatres closed and the players, like many other Londoners, had to take to the country.

Though players had a low social status, they enjoyed great popularity, and one of the favorite forms of entertainment at Court was the performance of plays. To be commanded to perform at Court conferred great prestige upon a company of players, and printers frequently noted that fact when they published plays. Several of Shakespeare's plays were performed before the sovereign, and Shakespeare himself undoubtedly acted in some of these plays.

REFERENCES FOR FURTHER READING

Many readers will want suggestions for further reading about Shakespeare and his times. The literature in this field is enormous but a few references will serve as guides to further study. A simple and useful little book is Gerald Sanders, *A Shakespeare Primer* (New York, 1950). *A Companion to Shakespeare Studies*, edited by Harley Granville-Barker and G. B. Harrison (Cambridge, Eng., 1934) is a valuable guide. More detailed but still not too voluminous to be confusing is Hazelton Spencer, *The Art and Life of William Shakespeare* (New York, 1940) which, like Sanders' handbook, contains a brief annotated list of useful books on various aspects of the subject. The most detailed and scholarly work providing complete factual information about Shakespeare is Sir Edmund Chambers, *William Shakespeare: A Study of Facts and Problems* (2 vols., Oxford, 1930). For detailed, factual information about the Elizabethan and seventeenth-century stages, the definitive reference works are Sir Edmund Chambers, *The Elizabethan Stage* (4 vols., Oxford, 1923) and Gerald E. Bentley, *The Jacobean and Caroline Stage* (5 vols., Oxford, 1941-1956). Alfred Harbage, *Shakespeare's Audience* (New York, 1941) throws light on the nature and tastes of the customers for whom Elizabethan dramatists wrote.

Although specialists disagree about details of stage construction, the reader will find essential information in John C. Adams, *The Globe Playhouse: Its Design and Equipment* (Barnes & Noble, 1961). A model of the

Globe playhouse by Dr. Adams is on permanent exhibition in the Folger Shakespeare Library in Washington, D.C. An excellent description of the architecture of the Globe is Irwin Smith, *Shakespeare's Globe Playhouse: A Modern Reconstruction in Text and Scale Drawings Based upon the Reconstruction of the Globe by John Cranford Adams* (New York, 1956). Another recent study of the physical characteristics of the Globe is C. Walter Hodges, *The Globe Restored* (London, 1953). An easily read history of the early theatres is J. Q. Adams, *Shakespearean Playhouses: A History of English Theatres from the Beginnings to the Restoration* (Boston, 1917).

The following titles on theatrical history will provide information about Shakespeare's plays in later periods: Alfred Harbage, *Theatre for Shakespeare* (Toronto, 1955), Esther Cloudman Dunn, *Shakespeare in America* (New York, 1939); George C. D. Odell, *Shakespeare from Betterton to Irving* (2 vols., London, 1921); Arthur Colby Sprague, *Shakespeare and the Actors: The Stage Business in His Plays* (1660–1905) (Cambridge, Mass., 1944) and *Shakespearian Players and Performances* (Cambridge, Mass., 1953) Leslie Hotson, *The Commonwealth and Restoration Stage* (Cambridge, Mass., 1928) Alwin Thaler, *Shakspere to Sheridan: A Book About the Theatre of Yesterday and To-day* (Cambridge, Mass., 1922); Ernest Bradlee Watson, *Sheridan to Robertson: A Study of the 19th-Century London Stage* (Cambridge, Mass., 1926) Enid Welsford, *The Court Masque* (Cambridge, Mass., 1927) is an excellent study of the characteristics of this form of entertainment.

Harley Granville-Barker, *Prefaces to Shakespeare* (5 vols., London, 1927–48) provides stimulating critical discussion of the plays. An older classic of criticism is Andrew C. Bradley, *Shakespearean Tragedy: Lectures on*

Hamlet, Othello, King Lear, Macbeth (London, 1904), which is now available in an inexpensive reprint (New York, 1955). Thomas M. Parrott, *Shakespearean Comedy* (New York, 1949) is scholarly and readable. Shakespeare's dramatizations of English history are examined in E. M. W. Tillyard, *Shakespeare's History Plays* (London, 1948), and Lily Bess Campbell, *Shakespeare's "Histories," Mirrors of Elizabethan Policy* (San Marino, Calif., 1947) contains a more technical discussion of the same subject.

The question of the authenticity of Shakespeare's plays arouses perennial attention. A book that demolishes the notion of hidden cryptograms in the plays is William F. Friedman and Elizebeth S. Friedman, *The Shakespearean Ciphers Examined* (New York, 1957). A succinct account of the various absurdities advanced to suggest the authorship of a multitude of candidates other than Shakespeare will be found in R. C. Churchill, *Shakespeare and His Betters* (Bloomington, Ind., 1959) and Frank W. Wadsworth, *The Poacher from Stratford: A Partial Account of the Controversy over the Authorship of Shakespeare's Plays* (Berkeley, Calif., 1958). An essay on the curious notions in the writings of the anti-Shakespeareans is that by Louis B. Wright, "The Anti-Shakespeare Industry and the Growth of Cults," *The Virginia Quarterly Review*, XXXV (1959), 289-303.

Reprints of some of the sources for Shakespeare's plays, including *Romeo and Juliet*, can be found in *Shakespeare's Library* (2 vols., 1850), edited by John Payne Collier, and *The Shakespeare Classics* (12 vols., 1907-26), edited by Israel Gollancz. A discussion of the sources of *Romeo and Juliet* will be found in most of the foregoing general works on Shakespeare's plays. Of particular value are Kenneth Muir, *Shakespeare's Sources: Comedies and Tragedies*

(London, 1957), and Geoffrey Bullough, *Narrative and Dramatic Sources of Shakespeare* (New York, 1957); the latter is the first volume in a new series reprinting the actual sources. A discussion of the story as legend will be found in Olin Harris Moore, *The Legend of Romeo and Juliet* (Columbus, Ohio, 1950). Further bibliographical clues are given in Samuel A. Tannenbaum and Dorothy R. Tannenbaum, *Shakspere's Romeo and Juliet, A Concise Bibliography* (New York, 1950), but the student should bear in mind that this bibliography is unselective and not altogether accurate.

Interesting pictures as well as new information about Shakespeare will be found in F. E. Halliday, *Shakespeare, a Pictorial Biography* (London, 1956). Allardyce Nicoll, *The Elizabethans* (Cambridge, Eng., 1957) contains a variety of illustrations for the period.

A brief, clear, and accurate account of Tudor history is S. T. Bindoff, *The Tudors*, in the Penguin series. A readable general history is G. M. Trevelyan, *The History of England*, first published in 1926 and available in many editions. G. M. Trevelyan, *English Social History*, first published in 1942 and also available in many editions, provides fascinating information about England in all periods. Sir John Neale, *Queen Elizabeth* (London, 1934) is the best study of the great Queen. Various aspects of life in the Elizabethan period are treated in Louis B. Wright, *Middle-Class Culture in Elizabethan England* (Chapel Hill, N. C., 1935; reprinted by Cornell University Press, 1958). *Shakespeare's England: An Account of the Life and Manners of His Age,* edited by Sidney Lee and C. T. Onions (2 vols., Oxford, 1916), provides a large amount of information on many aspects of life in the Elizabethan period. Additional information will be found in Muriel St. C. Byrne, *Elizabethan Life in Town and Country* (Barnes & Noble, 1961).

The Folger Shakespeare Library is currently publishing a series of illustrated pamphlets on various aspects of English life in the sixteenth and seventeenth centuries. The following titles are available: Dorothy E. Mason, *Music in Elizabethan England*; Craig R. Thompson, *The English Church in the Sixteenth Century*; Louis B. Wright, *Shakespeare's Theatre and the Dramatic Tradition*; Giles E. Dawson, *The Life of William Shakespeare*; Virginia A. LaMar, *English Dress in the Age of Shakespeare*; Craig R. Thompson, *The Bible in English, 1525-1611*; Craig R. Thompson, *Schools in Tudor England*; Craig R. Thompson, *Universities in Tudor England*.

[Dramatis Personae.

Chorus.

Escalus, Prince of Verona.
Paris, a young Count, kinsman to the *Prince*.
Montague, } heads of two hostile families.
Capulet, }
An old Man, kin to *Capulet*.
Romeo, son to *Montague*.
Mercutio, kinsman to the *Prince*, and friend to *Romeo*.
Benvolio, nephew to *Montague*, and friend to *Romeo*.
Tybalt, nephew to *Capulet's wife*.
Friar Laurence, } Franciscans.
Friar John, }
Balthasar, servant to *Romeo*.
Abram, servant to *Montague*.
Sampson, } servants to *Capulet*.
Gregory, }
Peter, servant to *Juliet's* nurse.
An Apothecary.
Three Musicians.
An Officer.

Montague's wife.
Capulet's wife.
Juliet, daughter to *Capulet*.
Nurse to *Juliet*.

Citizens of Verona; Gentlemen and Gentlewomen of both
houses; Maskers, Torchbearers, Pages, Guards, Watch-
men, Servants, and Attendants.

SCENE: *Verona; Mantua.*]

THE TRAGEDY OF
ROMEO AND JULIET

ACT I

[Pro. I.] 3. **mutiny:** riot.

4. **civil blood makes civil hands unclean:** citizens soil their hands with each other's blood. The contrast is with the spilling of blood by foreign invaders.

6. **star-crossed:** ill-destined; that is, born under unfavorable stars.

———————————

I. i. A street brawl between followers of the houses of Montague and Capulet reveals the feud between the two houses. Prince Escalus, ruler of Verona, is incensed at this latest disturbance of the peace by the Montagues and Capulets and warns that death will be the penalty for another such incident.

Young Romeo, heir of the Montague family, is melancholy over his unrequited love for Rosaline and cannot be consoled by his cousin Benvolio, who counsels him to compare his mistress' beauty with that of other women.

———————————

Ent. **bucklers:** small shields, also sometimes known as "targets."

1. **carry coals:** submit to humiliation.
2. **colliers:** workers or dealers in coal.
3. **an:** if; **in choler:** full of anger.

[THE PROLOGUE]

[Enter *Chorus*.]

Chor. Two households, both alike in dignity,
In fair Verona, where we lay our scene,
From ancient grudge break to new mutiny,
Where civil blood makes civil hands unclean.
From forth the fatal loins of these two foes   5
A pair of star-crossed lovers take their life,
Whose misadventured piteous overthrows
Doth with their death bury their parents' strife.
The fearful passage of their death-marked love,
And the continuance of their parents' rage,   10
Which, but their children's end, naught could remove,
Is now the two hours' traffic of our stage,
The which if you with patient ears attend,
What here shall miss, our toil shall strive to mend.

[*Exit.*]

ACT I

Scene I. [A street in Verona.]

Enter *Sampson* and *Gregory* (with swords and bucklers)
of the house of *Capulet*.

Samp. Gregory, on my word, we'll not carry coals.
Greg. No, for then we should be colliers.
Samp. I mean, an we be in choler, we'll draw.

4. **collar:** halter; i.e., hangman's noose.

11. **take the wall:** insist on being acknowledged the superior. The side nearest the house walls in cities of the time was usually cleaner because a drainage ditch frequently ran down the center of the streets. Courtesy to those of superior rank demanded that they be allowed to walk nearest the wall.

13. **goes to the wall:** proverbial, "is pushed to the rear."

30. **poor-John:** salted fish, poorly regarded as a food; **tool:** sword.

A young man with a sword and buckler.
From Braun and Hogenberg's Map of London (1554-58). **2**

Greg. Ay, while you live, draw your neck out of collar.

Samp. I strike quickly, being moved.   5

Greg. But thou art not quickly moved to strike.

Samp. A dog of the house of Montague moves me.

Greg. To move is to stir, and to be valiant is to stand.
Therefore, if thou art moved, thou runnest away.

Samp. A dog of that house shall move me to stand. I   10
will take the wall of any man or maid of Montague's.

Greg. That shows thee a weak slave, for the weakest
goes to the wall.

Samp. 'Tis true; and therefore women, being the
weaker vessels, are ever thrust to the wall. Therefore I   15
will push Montague's men from the wall and thrust his
maids to the wall.

Greg. The quarrel is between our masters and us their
men.

Samp. 'Tis all one. I will show myself a tyrant. When I   20
have fought with the men, I will be cruel with the maids:
I will cut off their heads.

Greg. The heads of the maids?

Samp. Ay, the heads of the maids, or their maiden-
heads. Take it in what sense thou wilt.   25

Greg. They must take it in sense that feel it.

Samp. Me they shall feel while I am able to stand; and
'tis known I am a pretty piece of flesh.

Greg. 'Tis well thou art not fish; if thou hadst, thou
hadst been poor-John. Draw thy tool! Here comes two of   30
the house of Montagues.

Enter two other *Servingmen* [*Abram* and *Balthasar*].

Samp. My naked weapon is out. Quarrel! I will back
thee.

36. **marry:** by the Virgin Mary; a mild oath.
39. **list:** please.
40. **bite my thumb:** an insulting gesture.
61. **swashing:** crashing.

A street brawl.
From Joost Damhouder, *Praxis rerum criminalium* (1570).

Greg. How? turn thy back and run?

Samp. Fear me not.   35

Greg. No, marry. I fear thee!

Samp. Let us take the law of our sides; let them begin.

Greg. I will frown as I pass by, and let them take it as
they list.

Samp. Nay, as they dare. I will bite my thumb at   40
them; which is disgrace to them, if they bear it.

Abr. Do you bite your thumb at us, sir?

Samp. I do bite my thumb, sir.

Abr. Do you bite your thumb at us, sir?

Samp. [*Aside to Gregory*] Is the law of our side if I   45
say ay?

Greg. [*Aside to Sampson*] No.

Samp. No, sir, I do not bite my thumb at you, sir; but
I bite my thumb, sir.

Greg. Do you quarrel, sir?   50

Abr. Quarrel, sir? No, sir.

Samp. But if you do, sir, I am for you. I serve as good
a man as you.

Abr. No better.

Samp. Well, sir.   55

Enter *Benvolio.*

Greg. [*Aside to Sampson*] Say "better." Here comes
one of my master's kinsmen.

Samp. Yes, better, sir.

Abr. You lie.

Samp. Draw, if you be men. Gregory, remember thy   60
swashing blow.   *They fight.*

Ben. Part, fools! [*Beats down their swords.*]
Put up your swords. You know not what you do.

A man with a pike.

From George Silver, *Paradoxes of Defence* (1599).

64-5. **heartless hinds:** timid servants, with a pun on "heart/hart."

71. **Have at thee:** on your guard.

S.D. before l. 72. **partisans:** pikes with small, double-edged blades.

72. **bills:** long-handled weapons with small blades flat on one side and ending in points, often hooked.

S.D. before l. 76. **gown:** that is, a dressing gown, though elderly men often wore full robes called "gowns" as regular street attire.

79. **spite:** defiance.

4

Enter *Tybalt*.

Tyb. What, art thou drawn among these heartless
    hinds?   65
Turn thee, Benvolio! look upon thy death.
    Ben. I do but keep the peace. Put up thy sword,
Or manage it to part these men with me.
    Tyb. What, drawn, and talk of peace? I hate the word
As I hate hell, all Montagues, and thee.   70
Have at thee, coward!   [*They*] *fight*.

Enter three or four *Citizens* with clubs or partisans
              [and an *Officer*].

Officer. Clubs, bills, and partisans! Strike! beat them
down!
    Citizens. Down with the Capulets! Down with the
Montagues!   75

Enter *Old Capulet* in his gown, and his *Wife*.

Cap. What noise is this? Give me my long sword, ho!
    Wife. A crutch, a crutch! Why call you for a sword?
    Cap. My sword, I say! Old Montague is come
And flourishes his blade in spite of me.

Enter *Old Montague* and his *Wife*.

Mon. Thou villain Capulet!—Hold me not, let me go.   80
    M. Wife. Thou shalt not stir one foot to seek a foe.

Enter *Prince Escalus*, with his *Train*.

Prince. Rebellious subjects, enemies to peace,
Profaners of this neighbor-stained steel—

94. **beseeming:** suitable.

96. **Cankered . . . cankered:** rusted . . . rankling.

98. **forfeit of the peace:** penalty for creating a disturbance.

105. **set this . . . quarrel new abroach:** opened the tap of enmity again.

A dueling stance.
From Angelo Vizani, *Trattato dello schermo* (1588).

Will they not hear? What, ho! you men, you beasts,
That quench the fire of your pernicious rage   85
With purple fountains issuing from your veins!
On pain of torture, from those bloody hands
Throw your mistempered weapons to the ground
And hear the sentence of your moved prince.
Three civil brawls, bred of an airy word   90
By thee, old Capulet, and Montague,
Have thrice disturbed the quiet of our streets
And made Verona's ancient citizens
Cast by their grave beseeming ornaments
To wield old partisans, in hands as old,   95
Cankered with peace, to part your cankered hate.
If ever you disturb our streets again,
Your lives shall pay the forfeit of the peace.
For this time all the rest depart away.
You, Capulet, shall go along with me;   100
And, Montague, come you this afternoon,
To know our farther pleasure in this case,
To old Freetown, our common judgment place.
Once more, on pain of death, all men depart.
     Exeunt [all but Montague, his Wife, and Benvolio].
     Mon. Who set this ancient quarrel new abroach?   105
Speak, nephew, were you by when it began?
     Ben. Here were the servants of your adversary
And yours, close fighting ere I did approach.
I drew to part them. In the instant came
The fiery Tybalt, with his sword prepared;   110
Which, as he breathed defiance to my ears,
He swung about his head and cut the winds,
Who, nothing hurt withal, hissed him in scorn.
While we were interchanging thrusts and blows,
Came more and more, and fought on part and part,   115
Till the Prince came, who parted either part.

Aurora.

From Vincenzo Cartari, *Imagini de gli dei delli antichi* (1615).

121. **drave:** drove.

126. **covert:** hiding place.

127. **affections:** inclinations; that is, his momentary mood.

137. **Aurora:** the goddess of the dawn.

138. **heavy:** sorrowful, depressed.

150. **close:** reticent.

M. Wife. O, where is Romeo? Saw you him today?
Right glad I am he was not at this fray.

   Ben. Madam, an hour before the worshiped sun
Peered forth the golden window of the East,   120
A troubled mind drave me to walk abroad,
Where, underneath the grove of sycamore
That westward rooteth from the city's side,
So early walking did I see your son.
Towards him I made, but he was ware of me   125
And stole into the covert of the wood.
I—measuring his affections by my own,
Which then most sought where most might not be found,
Being one too many by my weary self—
Pursued my humor, not pursuing his,   130
And gladly shunned who gladly fled from me.

   Mon. Many a morning hath he there been seen,
With tears augmenting the fresh morning's dew,
Adding to clouds more clouds with his deep sighs;
But all so soon as the all-cheering sun   135
Should in the farthest East begin to draw
The shady curtains from Aurora's bed,
Away from light steals home my heavy son
And private in his chamber pens himself,
Shuts up his windows, locks fair daylight out,   140
And makes himself an artificial night.
Black and portentous must this humor prove
Unless good counsel may the cause remove.

   Ben. My noble uncle, do you know the cause?

   Mon. I neither know it nor can learn of him.   145

   Ben. Have you importuned him by any means?

   Mon. Both by myself and many other friends;
But he, his own affections' counselor,
Is to himself—I will not say how true—
But to himself so secret and so close,   150

151. **sounding:** being sounded; i.e., understood.

152. **envious:** malicious.

153. **he:** it.

154. **sun:** Lewis Theobald's suggestion for "same" in the First Folio and Second Quarto.

159. **happy:** fortunate; **stay:** waiting.

160. **To hear true shrift:** as to hear a true confession.

172. **in his view:** in its glance.

173. **proof:** trial.

174. **whose view is muffled still:** whose sight is always blindfolded. Cupid, or Eros, was often pictured with a cloth tied over his eyes.

175. **his will:** its amorous desire.

178. **much to do:** a great commotion.

So far from sounding and discovery,
As is the bud bit with an envious worm
Ere he can spread his sweet leaves to the air
Or dedicate his beauty to the sun.
Could we but learn from whence his sorrows grow,   155
We would as willingly give cure as know.

Enter *Romeo*.

Ben. See, where he comes. So please you step aside,
I'll know his grievance, or be much denied.
Mon. I would thou wert so happy by thy stay
To hear true shrift. Come, madam, let's away.   160
                              Exeunt [Montague and Wife].
Ben. Good morrow, cousin.
Rom.   Is the day so young?
Ben. But new struck nine.
Rom.   Ay me! sad hours seem long.
Was that my father that went hence so fast?   165
Ben. It was. What sadness lengthens Romeo's hours?
Rom. Not having that which having makes them short.
Ben. In love?
Rom. Out—
Ben. Of love?   170
Rom. Out of her favor where I am in love.
Ben. Alas that love, so gentle in his view,
Should be so tyrannous and rough in proof!
Rom. Alas that love, whose view is muffled still,
Should without eyes see pathways to his will!   175
Where shall we dine?—O me! What fray was here?—
Yet tell me not, for I have heard it all.
Here's much to do with hate, but more with love.
Why then, O brawling love! O loving hate!
O anything, of nothing first create!   180

181. **vanity:** frivolity.

184 **Still-waking:** always wakeful.

185 **that feel no love in this:** that can take no pleasure in this love.

192 **prest:** oppressed, burdened.

196 **Being purged:** that is, the air being purged of the smoke.

201 **Soft:** wait a minute.

202 **An if:** if.

205. **sadness:** earnest truth; that is, without so much wordplay.

206. **groan:** Romeo puns on the word **sadness.**

208. **sadly:** gravely.

210. **ill urged:** It cannot be cheerful to a very sick person to be reminded of making his will.

O heavy lightness! serious vanity!
Misshapen chaos of well-seeming forms!
Feather of lead, bright smoke, cold fire, sick health!
Still-waking sleep, that is not what it is!
This love feel I, that feel no love in this.   185
Dost thou not laugh?
   Ben.   No, coz, I rather weep.
   Rom. Good heart, at what?
   Ben.   At thy good heart's oppression.
   Rom. Why, such is love's transgression.   190
Griefs of mine own lie heavy in my breast,
Which thou wilt propagate, to have it prest
With more of thine. This love that thou hast shown
Doth add more grief to too much of mine own.
Love is a smoke raised with the fume of sighs;   195
Being purged, a fire sparkling in lovers' eyes;
Being vexed, a sea nourished with lovers' tears.
What is it else? A madness most discreet,
A choking gall, and a preserving sweet.
Farewell, my coz.   200
   Ben.   Soft! I will go along.
An if you leave me so, you do me wrong.
   Rom. Tut! I have lost myself; I am not here:
This is not Romeo, he's some other where.
   Ben. Tell me in sadness, who is that you love?   205
   Rom. What, shall I groan and tell thee?
   Ben.   Groan? Why, no;
But sadly tell me who.
   Rom. Bid a sick man in sadness make his will.
Ah, word ill urged to one that is so ill!   210
In sadness, cousin, I do love a woman.
   Ben. I aimed so near when I supposed you loved.
   Rom. A right good markman! And she's fair I love.
   Ben. A right fair mark, fair coz, is soonest hit.

216. **Dian's wit:** the wisdom of the goddess Diana in preferring chastity.

217. **proof:** armor.

219. **stay:** endure.

221. **ope her lap to saint-seducing gold:** a reference to Zeus' seduction of Danäe in the form of a shower of gold.

224. **still:** forever; see l. 184.

228-29. **wisely too fair,/ To merit bliss by making me despair:** that is, she is wise in thinking of the reward of chastity, but her beauty is so great that her wise decision causes me to despair because my love will not be requited.

230. **forsworn to:** renounced.

237. **To call hers (exquisite) in question more:** looking at the beauty of other women merely impresses me more firmly with the exquisiteness of her beauty. To **call in question** is to review mentally.

238. **happy:** fortunate; see l. 159; **masks:** worn by women of fashion on public occasions.

242. **passing:** surpassingly.

243. **note:** reminder.

244. **passed:** surpassed.

246. **pay that doctrine, or else die in debt:** give that doctrine its due (i.e., make you acknowledge the merit of forgetting) or never give up the attempt until I die.

Rom. Well, in that hit you miss. She'll not be hit 215
With Cupid's arrow. She hath Dian's wit,
And, in strong proof of chastity well armed,
From Love's weak childish bow she lives unharmed.
She will not stay the siege of loving terms,
Nor bide the encounter of assailing eyes, 220
Nor ope her lap to saint-seducing gold.
O, she is rich in beauty; only poor
That, when she dies, with beauty dies her store.
  Ben. Then she hath sworn that she will still live chaste?
  Rom. She hath, and in that sparing makes huge waste; 225
For beauty, starved with her severity,
Cuts beauty off from all posterity.
She is too fair, too wise, wisely too fair,
To merit bliss by making me despair.
She hath forsworn to love, and in that vow 230
Do I live dead that live to tell it now.
  Ben. Be ruled by me: forget to think of her.
  Rom. O, teach me how I should forget to think!
  Ben. By giving liberty unto thine eyes:
Examine other beauties. 235
  Rom.   'Tis the way
To call hers (exquisite) in question more.
These happy masks that kiss fair ladies' brows,
Being black, puts us in mind they hide the fair.
He that is strucken blind cannot forget 240
The precious treasure of his eyesight lost.
Show me a mistress that is passing fair,
What doth her beauty serve but as a note
Where I may read who passed that passing fair?
Farewell. Thou canst not teach me to forget. 245
  Ben. I'll pay that doctrine, or else die in debt.

                         Exeunt.

I. [ii.] The County Paris asks Capulet for Juliet's hand. Capulet replies that Juliet, not yet fourteen, is too young for marriage, but promises his consent if Paris pleases her. He invites Paris to a party that night at which he may compare Juliet with other ladies and court her if he still rates her highest.

Capulet sends a servant with a list to invite friends and relatives, but the servant, unable to read himself, turns to Benvolio and Romeo, whom he meets in the street, to interpret it for him. Since Rosaline's name is among the invited guests, Benvolio suggests that they go to the ball so that Romeo may compare her with other beauties. Romeo agrees but reaffirms his eternal devotion to Rosaline.

▪▪▪▪▪▪▪▪▪▪▪▪▪▪▪▪▪▪▪▪▪▪▪▪

Ent. **County:** count.

14. **The earth hath swallowed all my hopes but she:** that is, she is his only living child.

15. **hopeful lady:** lady on whom all my hopes are pinned; **earth:** universe.

18. **An:** if; see I. i. 3.

18-9. **within her scope of choice/ Lies my consent:** that is, my consent is limited by her own wishes.

[Scene II. A street near the Capulet house.]

Enter *Capulet, County Paris,* and [*Servant*]—the *Clown.*

Cap. But Montague is bound as well as I,
In penalty alike; and 'tis not hard, I think,
For men so old as we to keep the peace.
    Par. Of honorable reckoning are you both,
And pity 'tis you lived at odds so long.   5
But now, my lord, what say you to my suit?
    Cap. But saying o'er what I have said before:
My child is yet a stranger in the world,
She hath not seen the change of fourteen years;
Let two more summers wither in their pride   10
Ere we may think her ripe to be a bride.
    Par. Younger than she are happy mothers made.
    Cap. And too soon marred are those so early made.
The earth hath swallowed all my hopes but she;
She is the hopeful lady of my earth.   15
But woo her, gentle Paris, get her heart;
My will to her consent is but a part.
An she agree, within her scope of choice
Lies my consent and fair according voice.
This night I hold an old accustomed feast,   20
Whereto I have invited many a guest,
Such as I love, and you among the store,
One more, most welcome, makes my number more.
At my poor house look to behold this night
Earth-treading stars that make dark heaven light.   25
Such comfort as do lusty young men feel
When well-appareled April on the heel
Of limping Winter treads, even such delight
Among fresh female buds shall you this night

30. **Inherit:** possess.

32-3. **Which, on more view of many, mine, being one,/ May stand in number, though in reck'ning none:** when so many beauties are viewed, my one among them may figure only statistically, not comparing with the others in beauty.

38. **on their pleasure stay:** await their pleasure.

40-2. **shoemaker . . . nets:** the confusion of professions and their tools is typical of the comic errors of clowns in Elizabethan drama; **meddle:** occupy himself: **yard:** yardstick.

45. **In good time:** an exclamation on seeing Romeo and Benvolio approach.

48. **holp:** helped. obsolete past tense.

52. **Your plantain leaf:** that is, plantain leaves in general, which were considered effective in staunching blood.

54. **broken:** wounded.

58. **God-den:** good evening.

Inherit at my house. Hear all, all see, 30
And like her most whose merit most shall be;
Which, on more view of many, mine, being one,
May stand in number, though in reck'ning none.
Come, go with me. [*To Servant, giving him a paper*] Go,
    sirrah, trudge about 35
Through fair Verona; find those persons out
Whose names are written there, and to them say,
My house and welcome on their pleasure stay.

                       Exeunt [*Capulet and Paris*].

   Serv. Find them out whose names are written here! It
is written that the shoemaker should meddle with his 40
yard and the tailor with his last, the fisher with his pencil
and the painter with his nets; but I am sent to find those
persons whose names are here writ, and can never find
what names the writing person hath here writ. I must to
the learned. In good time! 45

Enter *Benvolio* and *Romeo*.

   Ben. Tut, man, one fire burns out another's burning;
One pain is lessened by another's anguish;
Turn giddy, and be holp by backward turning;
One desperate grief cures with another's languish.
Take thou some new infection to thy eye, 50
And the rank poison of the old will die.
   Rom. Your plantain leaf is excellent for that.
   Ben. For what, I pray thee?
   Rom.   For your broken shin.
   Ben. Why, Romeo, art thou mad? 55
   Rom. Not mad, but bound more than a madman is;
Shut up in prison, kept without my food,
Whipped and tormented and—God-den, good fellow.
   Serv. God gi' go-den. I pray, sir, can you read?

64. **Rest you merry:** may you continue happy. Romeo's joking goes over the clown's head. He concludes that Romeo cannot read and prepares to seek someone who can.

85. **crush:** consume; a slang phrase.

87. **ancient:** "old accustomed"; see l. 20. Presumably this was a traditional celebration of an occasion of family importance.

90. **unattainted:** untainted, unbiased.

Old Capulet.
From Antonio Doni, *L'academia Peregrina e i mondi* (1552).

Rom. Ay, mine own fortune in my misery.   60

Serv. Perhaps you have learned it without book. But
I pray, can you read anything you see?

Rom. Ay, if I know the letters and the language.

Serv. Ye say honestly. Rest you merry!

Rom. Stay, fellow; I can read.   *He reads.*   65

"Signior Martino and his wife and daughters;
County Anselmo and his beauteous sisters;
The lady widow of Vitruvio;
Signior Placentio and his lovely nieces;
Mercutio and his brother Valentine;   70
Mine uncle Capulet, his wife, and daughters;
My fair niece Rosaline and Livia;
Signior Valentio and his cousin Tybalt;
Lucio and the lively Helena."

[*Gives back the paper.*] A fair assembly. Whither should   75
they come?

Serv. Up.

Rom. Whither?

Serv. To supper, to our house.

Rom. Whose house?   80

Serv. My master's.

Rom. Indeed I should have asked you that before.

Serv. Now I'll tell you without asking. My master is
the great rich Capulet; and if you be not of the house of
Montagues, I pray come and crush a cup of wine. Rest   85
you merry!   *Exit.*

Ben. At this same ancient feast of Capulet's
Sups the fair Rosaline whom thou so lovest,
With all the admired beauties of Verona.
Go thither, and with unattainted eye   90
Compare her face with some that I shall show,

95. **these:** i.e., these my eyes.

96. **Transparent:** easily seen through, as well as bright; **heretics:** breakers of traditional faith; i.e., because of changing his allegiance to Rosaline.

100. **poised:** weighed, compared.

102. **lady's love:** i.e., ladylove.

106. **splendor of mine own:** the beauty of the only woman for me.

▪▪▪▪▪▪▪▪▪▪▪▪▪▪▪▪▪▪▪▪▪▪▪▪▪▪▪▪▪▪▪▪▪▪▪▪▪

I. [iii.] Juliet's mother tells her of the County Paris' proposal of marriage. Juliet modestly disclaims any desire for marriage but promises to receive his attentions graciously.

▪▪▪▪▪▪▪▪▪▪▪▪▪▪▪▪▪▪▪▪▪▪▪▪▪▪

9. **give leave awhile:** excuse us for a little; a polite request to leave.

And I will make thee think thy swan a crow.
  Rom. When the devout religion of mine eye
Maintains such falsehood, then turn tears to fires;
And these, who, often drowned, could never die,   95
Transparent heretics, be burnt for liars!
One fairer than my love? The all-seeing sun
Ne'er saw her match since first the world begun.
  Ben. Tut! you saw her fair, none else being by,
Herself poised with herself in either eye;   100
But in that crystal scales let there be weighed
Your lady's love against some other maid
That I will show you shining at this feast,
And she shall scant show well that now shows best.
  Rom. I'll go along, no such sight to be shown,   105
But to rejoice in splendor of mine own.

                                     [*Exeunt.*]

[Scene III. Capulet's house.]

Enter *Capulet's Wife*, and *Nurse*.

  Wife. Nurse, where's my daughter? Call her forth to
    me.
  Nurse. Now, by my maidenhead at twelve year old,
I bade her come. What, lamb! what, ladybird!
God forbid! Where's this girl? What, Juliet!   5

Enter *Juliet*.

  Jul. How now? Who calls?
  Nurse. Your mother.
  Jul. Madam, I am here. What is your will?
  Wife. This is the matter—Nurse, give leave awhile,

11. **thou's:** thou shalt.

12. **a pretty age:** that is, approaching the age when marriage should be thought of.

16. **teen:** affliction.

18. **Lammastide:** August 1, a holy feast day.

26. **marry:** indeed; see I. i. 36.

33. **I do bear a brain:** I still have my wits about me.

37. **trow:** declare. The phrase means that she didn't need to be told to leave the quaking dovehouse.

40. **rood:** cross.

42. **even:** just; **broke her brow:** cut her forehead; see I. [ii.] 54.

We must talk in secret. Nurse, come back again;　　　10
I have remembered me, thou's hear our counsel.
Thou knowest my daughter's of a pretty age.

　Nurse. Faith, I can tell her age unto an hour.

　Wife. She's not fourteen.

　Nurse.　　　　　　　I'll lay fourteen of my teeth—　　15
And yet, to my teen be it spoken, I have but four—
She's not fourteen. How long is it now
To Lammastide?

　Wife.　　　　A fortnight and odd days.

　Nurse. Even or odd, of all days in the year,　　　20
Come Lammas Eve at night shall she be fourteen.
Susan and she (God rest all Christian souls!)
Were of an age. Well, Susan is with God;
She was too good for me. But, as I said,
On Lammas Eve at night shall she be fourteen;　　25
That shall she, marry; I remember it well.
'Tis since the earthquake now eleven years;
And she was weaned (I never shall forget it),
Of all the days of the year, upon that day;
For I had then laid wormwood to my dug,　　　30
Sitting in the sun under the dovehouse wall.
My lord and you were then at Mantua—
Nay, I do bear a brain—But, as I said,
When it did taste the wormwood on the nipple
Of my dug and felt it bitter, pretty fool,　　　35
To see it tetchy and fall out with the dug!
Shake, quoth the dovehouse! 'Twas no need, I trow,
To bid me trudge.
And since that time it is eleven years,
For then she could stand alone; nay, by the rood,　40
She could have run and waddled all about;
For even the day before, she broke her brow;
And then my husband (God be with his soul!

A girl with a duenna.
From Giovanni Astolfi, *Della officina istoria* (1622).

44. **'A:** he.

47. **by my holidam: holidam** or "halidom" in earlier times was the name given to a holy relic. The word later became popularly confused with "holy dame" and was thought to refer to the Virgin. Shakespeare always used the phrase as a mild oath.

52. **stinted:** stopped (crying).

56. **it:** its.

76-7. **much upon these years/ That:** at about the same age as.

'A was a merry man) took up the child.
"Yea," quoth he, "dost thou fall upon thy face?   45
Thou wilt fall backward when thou hast more wit,
Wilt thou not, Jule?" and, by my holidam,
The pretty wretch left crying, and said "Ay."
To see now how a jest shall come about!
I warrant, an I should live a thousand years,   50
I never should forget it. "Wilt thou not, Jule?" quoth he,
And, pretty fool, it stinted, and said "Ay."
    Wife. Enough of this. I pray thee hold thy peace.
    Nurse. Yes, madam. Yet I cannot choose but laugh
To think it should leave crying and say "Ay."   55
And yet, I warrant, it had upon it brow
A bump as big as a young cock'rel's stone;
A perilous knock; and it cried bitterly.
"Yea," quoth my husband, "fallst upon thy face?
Thou wilt fall backward when thou comest to age,   60
Wilt thou not, Jule?" It stinted, and said "Ay."
    Jul. And stint thou too, I pray thee, nurse, say I.
    Nurse. Peace, I have done. God mark thee to his grace!
Thou wast the prettiest babe that e'er I nursed.
An I might live to see thee married once,   65
I have my wish.
    Wife. Marry, that "marry" is the very theme
I came to talk of. Tell me, daughter Juliet,
How stands your disposition to be married?
    Jul. It is an honor that I dream not of.   70
    Nurse. An honor? Were not I thine only nurse,
I would say thou hadst sucked wisdom from thy teat.
    Wife. Well, think of marriage now. Younger than you,
Here in Verona, ladies of esteem,
Are made already mothers. By my count,   75
I was your mother much upon these years
That you are now a maid. Thus then in brief:

80. **a man of wax:** a very model of a man; that is, as beautiful as an artist's figure of a man in wax.

87. **several:** separate.

88. **one another lends content:** each feature lends a more pleasing aspect to the other.

89-90. **what obscured in this fair volume lies/ Find written in the margent of his eyes:** what you cannot tell of his character from his features his eyes will make clear. The **margent** (margin) was the usual place for explanatory notes in books of the time.

92. **cover:** probably a double meaning: something which enfolds him (as in a wifely embrace), and something which confines him.

93-4 **The fish lives in the sea, and 'tis much pride/ For fair without the fair within to hide:** the fish in the sea make a splendid sight—one beautiful thing containing another of equal beauty.

101. **I'll look to like, if looking liking move:** i.e., I am prepared to look favorably upon him, if mere sight is considered sufficient to produce affection.

107. **straight:** at once.

The valiant Paris seeks you for his love.
  Nurse. A man, young lady! lady, such a man
As all the world—why he's a man of wax.   80
  Wife. Verona's summer hath not such a flower.
  Nurse. Nay, he's a flower, in faith—a very flower.
  Wife. What say you? Can you love the gentleman?
This night you shall behold him at our feast.
Read o'er the volume of young Paris' face,   85
And find delight writ there with beauty's pen;
Examine every several lineament,
And see how one another lends content;
And what obscured in this fair volume lies
Find written in the margent of his eyes.   90
This precious book of love, this unbound lover,
To beautify him only lacks a cover.
The fish lives in the sea, and 'tis much pride
For fair without the fair within to hide.
That book in many's eyes doth share the glory,   95
That in gold clasps locks in the golden story;
So shall you share all that he doth possess,
By having him making yourself no less.
  Nurse. No less? Nay, bigger! Women grow by men.
  Wife. Speak briefly, can you like of Paris' love?   100
  Jul. I'll look to like, if looking liking move;
But no more deep will I endart mine eye
Than your consent gives strength to make it fly.

Enter a *Servingman.*

  Serv. Madam, the guests are come, supper served up,
you called, my young lady asked for, the nurse cursed in 105
the pantry, and everything in extremity. I must hence to
wait. I beseech you follow straight.

109. **stays:** awaits you; see I. [ii.] 38.

░░░░░░░░░░░░░░░░░░░░░░░░░░░░░░░░░░

I. [iv.] Romeo, Benvolio, and their friend Mercutio are on their way to the Capulets' celebration. They are disguised in masking costume to escape recognition Mercutio, a young man of irrepressible high spirits, entertains them with a description of the tiny queen of fairies, but Romeo is bored by Mercutio and expresses a feeling of foreboding at the rash prank of attending their enemy's festivities.

░░░░░░░░░░░░░░░░░░░░░░░░░░░░

1. **shall this speech be spoke for our excuse:** shall we make a formal introduction of our group of maskers (as was the old-fashioned custom).

3. **The date is out of such prolixity:** such wordiness is out-of-date.

4. **Cupid:** a typical conceit for the speaker of such polite introductions; **hoodwinked:** blindfolded.

6. **crowkeeper:** a boy stationed to protect the fields from crows with a bow and arrows.

7. **without-book:** impromptu.

12. **heavy:** sad; see I. i. 138.

18. **bound:** (1) leap; (2) limit. Many dances of the day had leaping steps.

19. **sore:** sorely, painfully.

21. **a pitch:** i.e., any distance at all.

Wife. We follow thee. *Exit* [*Servingman*]. Juliet, the
    County stays.
Nurse. Go, girl, seek happy nights to happy days.   110
                     Exeunt.

[Scene IV. A street near the Capulet house.]

Enter Romeo, Mercutio, Benvolio, with five or six other
Maskers; Torchbearers.

Rom. What, shall this speech be spoke for our excuse?
Or shall we on without apology?
Ben. The date is out of such prolixity.
We'll have no Cupid hoodwinked with a scarf,
Bearing a Tartar's painted bow of lath,   5
Scaring the ladies like a crowkeeper;
Nor no without-book prologue, faintly spoke
After the prompter, for our entrance;
But, let them measure us by what they will,
We'll measure them a measure, and be gone.   10
Rom. Give me a torch. I am not for this ambling;
Being but heavy, I will bear the light.
Mer. Nay, gentle Romeo, we must have you dance.
Rom. Not I, believe me. You have dancing shoes
With nimble soles; I have a soul of lead   15
So stakes me to the ground I cannot move.
Mer. You are a lover. Borrow Cupid's wings
And soar with them above a common bound.
Rom. I am too sore enpierced with his shaft
To soar with his light feathers, and so bound   20
I cannot bound a pitch above dull woe.
Under love's heavy burden do I sink.

30. **visor:** mask.

31. **curious:** careful, accurate. Though the modern sense was one of the earliest senses in which the word was used, Shakespeare always uses it in the sense of "finicky, fastidious, intricate," never in the sense of "prying"; **quote:** report.

35. **wantons:** sports, those disposed to gaiety.

36. **senseless:** incapable of feeling; **rushes:** usually used to cover floors at this time.

37. **proverbed with a grandsire phrase:** counseled by an old proverb.

39. **done:** (1) dun (dark); (2) finished.

40. **dun's the mouse, the constable's own word:** Mercutio continues to play on the word **done**. **Dun's the mouse** was a proverbial phrase cautioning the hearer to "keep dark" or "hidden"—a suitable motto for a constable who hoped to catch a suspect. Mercutio refers to Romeo's offer to be a candle-holder, which would call more attention to his presence.

41. **Dun:** the name for a horse in the proverb: "Dun is in the mire."

42. **save your reverence:** begging your pardon; a facetiously polite apology for comparing **love** with **mire**.

43. **burn daylight:** Mercutio means "waste time," "lose our opportunity," but Romeo continues their exchange of wit by misinterpreting him.

47. **good:** correct.

48. **that:** i.e., correct understanding.

52. **tonight:** last night.

Mer. And, to sink in it, should you burden love—
Too great oppression for a tender thing.

Rom. Is love a tender thing? It is too rough,   25
Too rude, too boist'rous, and it pricks like thorn.

Mer. If love be rough with you, be rough with love.
Prick love for pricking, and you beat love down.
Give me a case to put my visage in.
A visor for a visor! What care I   30
What curious eye doth quote deformities?
Here are the beetle brows shall blush for me.

Ben. Come, knock and enter, and no sooner in
But every man betake him to his legs.

Rom. A torch for me! Let wantons light of heart   35
Tickle the senseless rushes with their heels;
For I am proverbed with a grandsire phrase,
I'll be a candle-holder and look on;
The game was ne'er so fair, and I am done.

Mer. Tut! dun's the mouse, the constable's own word!   40
If thou art Dun, we'll draw thee from the mire
Of, save your reverence, love, wherein thou stickst
Up to the ears. Come, we burn daylight, ho!

Rom. Nay, that's not so.

Mer.   I mean, sir, in delay   45
We waste our lights in vain, like lamps by day.
Take our good meaning, for our judgment sits
Five times in that ere once in our five wits.

Rom. And we mean well, in going to this masque;
But 'tis no wit to go.   50

Mer.   Why, may one ask?

Rom. I dreamt a dream tonight.

Mer.   And so did I.

Rom. Well, what was yours?

Mer.   That dreamers often lie.   55

Rom. In bed asleep, while they do dream things true.

57. **Queen Mab:** queen of the fairies.

59. **agate stone:** gem stone for a ring.

72. **joiner:** cabinetmaker.

76. **straight:** immediately; see I. [iii.] 107; **on:** of.

82. **suit:** i.e., a petition for some preferment to the monarch, which the courtier might second for a proper reward.

83. **tithe-pig:** a pig due the parson as part of a parishioner's customary contribution.

85. **benefice:** living; post with an assured income.

Mer. O, then I see Queen Mab hath been with you.
She is the fairies' midwife, and she comes
In shape no bigger than an agate stone
On the forefinger of an alderman,   60
Drawn with a team of little atomies
Athwart men's noses as they lie asleep;
Her wagon spokes made of long spinners' legs,
The cover, of the wings of grasshoppers;
Her traces, of the smallest spider's web;   65
Her collars, of the moonshine's wat'ry beams;
Her whip, of cricket's bone; the lash, of film;
Her wagoner, a small grey-coated gnat,
Not half so big as a round little worm
Pricked from the lazy finger of a maid;   70
Her chariot is an empty hazelnut,
Made by the joiner squirrel or old grub,
Time out o' mind the fairies' coachmakers.
And in this state she gallops night by night
Through lovers' brains, and then they dream of love;   75
O'er courtiers' knees, that dream on curtsies straight;
O'er lawyers' fingers, who straight dream on fees;
O'er ladies' lips, who straight on kisses dream,
Which oft the angry Mab with blisters plagues,
Because their breaths with sweetmeats tainted are.   80
Sometime she gallops o'er a courtier's nose,
And then dreams he of smelling out a suit;
And sometime comes she with a tithe-pig's tail
Tickling a parson's nose as 'a lies asleep,
Then dreams he of another benefice.   85
Sometime she driveth o'er a soldier's neck,
And then dreams he of cutting foreign throats,
Of breaches, ambuscadoes, Spanish blades,
Of healths five fathom deep; and then anon

94. **elflocks:** matted hair from lack of proper grooming. Such unkempt hair was sometimes blamed on elves.

104. **fantasy:** fancy.

109. **dew-dropping South:** i.e., the rainy South wind.

112. **misgives:** forbodes.

113. **consequence:** event to come.

114. **his:** its.

S.D after l. 120. **They march . . . :** the scene break here is traditional with modern editions but the early texts indicate continuous action by the stage direction "They . . . stage, and Servingmen come forth. . . ." Similarly, the stage direction for the entrance of Capulet and his guests indicates that Romeo and his party are already on stage.

Drums in his ear, at which he starts and wakes,   90
And being thus frighted, swears a prayer or two
And sleeps again. This is that very Mab
That plaits the manes of horses in the night
And bakes the elflocks in foul sluttish hairs,
Which once untangled much misfortune bodes.   95
This is the hag, when maids lie on their backs,
That presses them and learns them first to bear,
Making them women of good carriage.
This is she—
    Rom.   Peace, peace, Mercutio, peace!   100
Thou talkst of nothing.
    Mer.   True, I talk of dreams;
Which are the children of an idle brain,
Begot of nothing but vain fantasy;
Which is as thin of substance as the air,   105
And more inconstant than the wind, who woos
Even now the frozen bosom of the North
And, being angered, puffs away from thence,
Turning his face to the dew-dropping South.
    Ben. This wind you talk of blows us from ourselves.   110
Supper is done, and we shall come too late.
    Rom. I fear, too early; for my mind misgives
Some consequence, yet hanging in the stars,
Shall bitterly begin his fearful date
With this night's revels and expire the term   115
Of a despised life, closed in my breast,
By some vile forfeit of untimely death.
But he that hath the steerage of my course
Direct my sail! On, lusty gentlemen!
    Ben. Strike, drum.   120
        They march about the stage. [*Exeunt.*]

I. [v.] Romeo and his party are greeted courteously by Capulet and his guests. Music is ordered and the guests dance. Romeo, standing aside to watch, is soon struck with admiration for the beauty of one girl. Tybalt of the house of Capulet hears him questioning a servant about her and recognizes his voice. Only a stern rebuke by Capulet prevents Tybalt from provoking a fight with Romeo.

At the first opportunity Romeo approaches the girl and their brief conversation kindles ardent love in both of them. Not until after they have parted do they learn that they are the heirs of the rival families.

<hr>

2. **trencher:** wooden platter.

5. **joint-stools:** sturdy stools made by a cabinetmaker.

5-6. **court-cupboard:** sideboard.

7. **marchpane:** marzipan, a confection of almond paste.

18. **Am I come near ye now:** am I hitting close to home.

24. **A hall:** that is, make room for dancing.

[Scene V. Capulet's house.]

Servingmen come forth with napkins.

1. Serv. Where's Potpan, that he helps not to take
away? He shift a trencher! he scrape a trencher!

2. Serv. When good manners shall lie all in one or two
men's hands, and they unwashed too, 'tis a foul thing.

1. Serv. Away with the joint-stools, remove the court-   5
cupboard, look to the plate. Good thou, save me a piece
of marchpane and, as thou lovest me, let the porter let in
Susan Grindstone and Nell. Anthony, and Potpan!

2. Serv. Ay, boy, ready.

1. Serv. You are looked for and called for, asked for   10
and sought for, in the great chamber.

3. Serv. We cannot be here and there too. Cheerly,
boys! Be brisk awhile, and the longer liver take all.

                         Exeunt.

[*Maskers* appear with *Capulet,* his *Wife, Juliet,* all the
                 Guests, and *Servants.*]

    Cap. Welcome, gentlemen! Ladies that have their toes
Unplagued with corns will have a bout with you.   15
Ah ha, my mistresses! which of you all
Will now deny to dance? She that makes dainty,
She I'll swear hath corns. Am I come near ye now?
Welcome, gentlemen! I have seen the day
That I have worn a visor and could tell   20
A whispering tale in a fair lady's ear,
Such as would please. 'Tis gone, 'tis gone, 'tis gone!
You are welcome, gentlemen! Come, musicians, play.
A hall, a hall! give room! and foot it, girls.

               Music plays, and they dance.

25. **turn the tables up:** that is, the leaves of the tables, which could be turned down out of the way when not needed.

27. **sirrah:** a term of address indicating familiarity; **this unlooked-for sport:** the feast was an "old accustomed one"; Capulet refers to the coming of the uninvited maskers.

28. **cousin:** the relative addressed is not necessarily literally a cousin; the term was used of any relative less close in blood than brother or sister of the speaker.

37. **elder:** that is, older than twenty-five years of age.

40. **ward:** minor.

55. **should:** must. Apparently Tybalt recognizes Romeo's voice.

57. **antic:** grotesque, referring to his mask.

58. **fleer:** mock; **solemnity:** festivity.

More light, you knaves! and turn the tables up,   25
And quench the fire, the room is grown too hot.
Ah, sirrah, this unlooked-for sport comes well.
Nay, sit, nay, sit, good cousin Capulet,
For you and I are past our dancing days.
How long is't now since last yourself and I   30
Were in a mask?
    2. Cap.   By'r Lady, thirty years.
    Cap. What, man? 'Tis not so much, 'tis not so much!
'Tis since the nuptial of Lucentio,
Come Pentecost as quickly as it will,   35
Some five-and-twenty years, and then we masked.
    2. Cap. 'Tis more, 'tis more! His son is elder, sir;
His son is thirty.
    Cap.   Will you tell me that?
His son was but a ward two years ago.   40
    Rom. [*To a Servingman*] What lady's that, which doth
    enrich the hand
Of yonder knight?
    Serv. I know not, sir.
    Rom. O, she doth teach the torches to burn bright!   45
It seems she hangs upon the cheek of night
Like a rich jewel in an Ethiop's ear—
Beauty too rich for use, for earth too dear!
So shows a snowy dove trooping with crows
As yonder lady o'er her fellows shows.   50
The measure done, I'll watch her place of stand
And, touching hers, make blessed my rude hand.
Did my heart love till now? Forswear it, sight!
For I ne'er saw true beauty till this night.
    Tyb. This, by his voice, should be a Montague.   55
Fetch me my rapier, boy. What, dares the slave
Come hither, covered with an antic face,
To fleer and scorn at our solemnity?

69. **portly:** dignified.

76. **Show a fair presence:** that is, put a good face on it.

77. **ill-beseeming semblance:** unbecoming appearance; see I. i. 94.

78. **It:** i.e., such a frowning look; **fits:** is suitable.

81. **goodman boy:** Capulet is losing his patience and addresses Tybalt as he would an inferior in both age and rank **Go to:** be off, that's enough.

83. **God shall mend my soul:** God save me; an exclamation of impatience.

84. **mutiny:** commotion, riot; see [Pro. I.] 3.

85. **set cock-a-hoop:** throw away all restraint. The phrase refers to opening the tap of a keg of liquor so that it flows continuously.

89. **scathe:** harm; **what:** what I'm doing.

91. **hearts:** hearties. Capulet is admiring the skill of the dancers; **princox:** an overbearing and vain youngster.

Now, by the stock and honor of my kin,
To strike him dead I hold it not a sin.   60
  Cap. Why, how now, kinsman? Wherefore storm you
    so?
  Tyb. Uncle, this is a Montague, our foe;
A villain, that is hither come in spite
To scorn at our solemnity this night.   65
  Cap. Young Romeo is it?
  Tyb.   'Tis he, that villain Romeo.
  Cap. Content thee, gentle coz, let him alone.
'A bears him like a portly gentleman,
And, to say truth, Verona brags of him   70
To be a virtuous and well-governed youth.
I would not for the wealth of all this town
Here in my house do him disparagement.
Therefore be patient, take no note of him.
It is my will; the which if thou respect,   75
Show a fair presence and put off these frowns,
An ill-beseeming semblance for a feast.
  Tyb. It fits when such a villain is a guest.
I'll not endure him.
  Cap.   He shall be endured.   80
What, goodman boy? I say he shall. Go to!
Am I the master here, or you? Go to!
You'll not endure him? God shall mend my soul!
You'll make a mutiny among my guests!
You will set cock-a-hoop! you'll be the man!   85
  Tyb. Why, uncle, 'tis a shame.
  Cap.   Go to, go to!
You are a saucy boy. Is't so, indeed?
This trick may chance to scathe you. I know what.
You must contrary me! Marry, 'tis time.—   90
Well said, my hearts!—You are a princox—go!

A religious pilgrim.
From Jacopo Caviceo, *Libro del peregrino* (1526).

94. **Patience perforce:** enforced restraint; a proverbial phrase.

95. **different greeting:** opposition.

99. **fine:** emendation by Lewis Warburton of the early reading "sin."

105. **palmer:** a pilgrim to religious shrines.

110. **Saints do not move, though grant for prayers' sake:** saints do not voluntarily intercede in human affairs but they may be moved to action by prayer.

116. **by the book:** according to formal rules, as though he had studied the art.

124. **shall have the chinks:** become rich, in view of her father's wealth.

Be quiet, or—More light, more light!—For shame!
I'll make you quiet; what!—Cheerly, my hearts!

Tyb. Patience perforce with willful choler meeting
Makes my flesh tremble in their different greeting.   95
I will withdraw; but this intrusion shall,
Now seeming sweet, convert to bitter gall.   *Exit.*

Rom. If I profane with my unworthiest hand
This holy shrine, the gentle fine is this:
My lips, two blushing pilgrims, ready stand   100
To smooth that rough touch with a tender kiss.

Jul. Good pilgrim, you do wrong your hand too much,
Which mannerly devotion shows in this;
For saints have hands that pilgrims' hands do touch,
And palm to palm is holy palmers' kiss.   105

Rom. Have not saints lips, and holy palmers too?

Jul. Ay, pilgrim, lips that they must use in prayer.

Rom. O, then, dear saint, let lips do what hands do!
They pray; grant thou, lest faith turn to despair.

Jul. Saints do not move, though grant for prayers' sake. 110

Rom. Then move not while my prayer's effect I take.
Thus from my lips, by thine my sin is purged. [*Kisses her.*]

Jul. Then have my lips the sin that they have took.

Rom. Sin from my lips? O trespass sweetly urged!
Give me my sin again.   [*Kisses her.*] 115

Jul.   You kiss by the book.

Nurse. Madam, your mother craves a word with you.

Rom. What is her mother?

Nurse.   Marry, bachelor,
Her mother is the lady of the house.   120
And a good lady, and a wise and virtuous.
I nursed her daughter that you talked withal.
I tell you, he that can lay hold of her
Shall have the chinks.

Rom.   Is she a Capulet?   125

126. **dear:** costly.

127. **the sport is at the best:** see I. [iv.] 39, where the same proverbial idea is expressed.

130. **towards:** in the offing, coming up.

135. **fay:** faith.

149. **Prodigious:** abnormal, like a freak; hence promising bad luck.

Death and lovers.
From Fabio Glissenti, *Discorsi morali contra il dispiacer del morire* (1600).

O dear account! my life is my foe's debt.

   Ben. Away, be gone, the sport is at the best.

   Rom. Ay, so I fear; the more is my unrest.

   Cap. Nay, gentlemen, prepare not to be gone;

We have a trifling foolish banquet towards.   130

                        They whisper in his ear.

Is it e'en so? Why then, I thank you all.

I thank you, honest gentlemen. Good night.

More torches here! [*Exeunt Maskers.*] Come on then, let's
    to bed.

Ah, sirrah, by my fay, it waxes late;   135

I'll to my rest.   *Exeunt [all but Juliet and Nurse].*

   Jul. Come hither, nurse. What is yond gentleman?

   Nurse. The son and heir of old Tiberio.

   Jul. What's he that now is going out of door?

   Nurse. Marry, that, I think, be young Petruchio.   140

   Jul. What's he that follows there, that would not dance?

   Nurse. I know not.

   Jul. Go ask his name.—If he be married,

My grave is like to be my wedding bed.

   Nurse. His name is Romeo, and a Montague,   145

The only son of your great enemy.

   Jul. My only love, sprung from my only hate!

Too early seen unknown, and known too late!

Prodigious birth of love it is to me

That I must love a loathed enemy.   150

   Nurse. What's this? what's this?

   Jul.   A rhyme I learnt even now

Of one I danced withal.

                One calls within, "Juliet."

   Nurse.   Anon, anon!   155

Come, let's away; the strangers all are gone.

                       Exeunt.

THE TRAGEDY OF
ROMEO AND JULIET

ACT II

[Pro. II.] 3. **fair:** lovely lady.

4. **matched:** compared.

⁊⁊⁊⁊⁊⁊⁊⁊⁊⁊⁊⁊⁊⁊⁊⁊⁊

[II. i.] Since Romeo now knows that Juliet is of the Capulet household, he is loath to leave their grounds. He leaps a wall and eludes his friends, who seek him in vain; Mercutio continues to make ribald jests at his expense.

⁊⁊⁊⁊⁊⁊⁊⁊⁊⁊⁊⁊⁊

2. **earth:** his own body; **center:** heart (i.e., Juliet).

[PROLOGUE]

[Enter *Chorus*.]

Chor. Now old desire doth in his deathbed lie,
And young affection gapes to be his heir;
That fair for which love groaned for and would die,
With tender Juliet matched, is now not fair.
Now Romeo is beloved, and loves again,　　　　　　　　5
Alike bewitched by the charm of looks;
But to his foe supposed he must complain,
And she steal love's sweet bait from fearful hooks.
Being held a foe, he may not have access
To breathe such vows as lovers use to swear,　　　　10
And she as much in love, her means much less
To meet her new beloved anywhere;
But passion lends them power, time means, to meet,
Temp'ring extremities with extreme sweet.

　　　　　　　　　　　　　　　　　　　　　[*Exit.*]

[ACT II]

[Scene I. A lane by the wall of Capulet's orchard.]

Enter *Romeo* alone.

Rom. Can I go forward when my heart is here?
Turn back, dull earth, and find thy center out.
　　　　　[*Climbs the wall and leaps down within it.*]

26

8. **conjure:** call him up by magic, as a sorcerer might raise a spirit.

13. **gossip:** confidant.

14. **purblind:** completely blind.

15. **Adam Cupid:** in giving **Cupid** a first name of **Adam,** Shakespeare is probably remembering a famous archer "Adam Bell," who is the hero of a popular ballad. **Adam** is an emendation first suggested in the eighteenth century for "Abraham" in the early texts.

16. **King Cophetua:** an old ballad tells of Cupid's wounding King Cophetua and causing him to love the beggar maid at first sight.

18. **The ape is dead:** Romeo, lying low, is compared to a trained ape who plays dead until his master gives the word.

22. **demesnes:** regions.

29. **were:** would be; **spite:** harm; see I. i. 79.

30. **fair:** proper; **honest:** honorable.

33. **be consorted with:** harmonize with; **humorous:** moist. In the sixteenth century, one of the meanings of the word "humor" was "damp exhalation." It also meant any fluid or juice of an animal or plant.

Enter *Benvolio* with *Mercutio*.

Ben. Romeo! my cousin Romeo! Romeo!
Mer.   He is wise,
And, on my life, hath stol'n him home to bed.   5
Ben. He ran this way, and leapt this orchard wall.
Call, good Mercutio.
Mer.   Nay, I'll conjure too.
Romeo! humors! madman! passion! lover!
Appear thou in the likeness of a sigh;   10
Speak but one rhyme, and I am satisfied!
Cry but "Ay me!" pronounce but "love" and "dove";
Speak to my gossip Venus one fair word,
One nickname for her purblind son and heir,
Young Adam Cupid, he that shot so trim   15
When King Cophetua loved the beggar maid!
He heareth not, he stirreth not, he moveth not;
The ape is dead, and I must conjure him.
I conjure thee by Rosaline's bright eyes,
By her high forehead and her scarlet lip,   20
By her fine foot, straight leg, and quivering thigh,
And the demesnes that there adjacent lie,
That in thy likeness thou appear to us!
Ben. An if he hear thee, thou wilt anger him.
Mer. This cannot anger him. 'Twould anger him   25
To raise a spirit in his mistress' circle
Of some strange nature, letting it there stand
Till she had laid it and conjured it down.
That were some spite; my invocation
Is fair and honest: in his mistress' name,   30
I conjure only but to raise up him.
Ben. Come, he hath hid himself among these trees
To be consorted with the humorous night.
Blind is his love and best befits the dark.

36. **medlar:** fruit resembling a small, brown apple, eaten only when nearly rotten.

41. **truckle bed:** trundle bed, such as children slept on, which might be stored under an adult bed when not in use.

<hr>

[**II. ii.**] Romeo overhears Juliet in her bedroom window declare her love for him and her despair that he is a Montague. They exchange vows of love, and Juliet promises to send a messenger to Romeo the next day to learn of his plans for their immediate marriage.

<hr>

Note: This scene break, though not a logical one, has become conventional; we have retained it merely because it is accepted generally and the scene numbering of the rest of the act would be affected in a way that might cause confusion of reference if we departed from the convention. Note that Romeo obviously overhears Benvolio and Mercutio and that lines 45 of Scene i and 1 of Scene ii form a couplet.

<hr>

8. **vestal livery:** virginal uniform.

Mer. If love be blind, love cannot hit the mark. 35
Now will he sit under a medlar tree
And wish his mistress were that kind of fruit
As maids call medlars when they laugh alone.
O, Romeo, that she were, O that she were
An open et cetera, thou a pop'rin pear! 40
Romeo, good night. I'll to my truckle bed;
This field-bed is too cold for me to sleep.
Come, shall we go?
 Ben.   Go then, for 'tis in vain
To seek him here that means not to be found. 45

        Exeunt.

[Scene II. Capulet's orchard.]

[Enter *Romeo.*]

Rom. He jests at scars that never felt a wound.

[Enter *Juliet* above at a window.]

But soft! What light through yonder window breaks?
It is the East, and Juliet is the sun!
Arise, fair sun, and kill the envious moon,
Who is already sick and pale with grief 5
That thou her maid art far more fair than she.
Be not her maid, since she is envious;
Her vestal livery is but sick and green,
And none but fools do wear it; cast it off.
It is my lady; O, it is my love! 10
O that she knew she were!
She speaks, yet she says nothing. What of that?
Her eye discourses; I will answer it.

35. **wherefore:** why.

I am too bold; 'tis not to me she speaks.
Two of the fairest stars in all the heaven,   15
Having some business, do entreat her eyes
To twinkle in their spheres till they return.
What if her eyes were there, they in her head?
The brightness of her cheek would shame those stars
As daylight doth a lamp; her eyes in heaven   20
Would through the airy region stream so bright
That birds would sing and think it were not night.
See how she leans her cheek upon her hand!
O that I were a glove upon that hand,
That I might touch that cheek!   25

    Jul.   Ay me!
    Rom.   She speaks.
O, speak again, bright angel! for thou art
As glorious to this night. being o'er my head,
As is a winged messenger of heaven   30
Unto the white-upturned wond'ring eyes
Of mortals that fall back to gaze on him
When he bestrides the lazy-pacing clouds
And sails upon the bosom of the air.

    Jul. O Romeo, Romeo! wherefore art thou Romeo?   35
Deny thy father and refuse thy name!
Or, if thou wilt not, be but sworn my love,
And I'll no longer be a Capulet.

    Rom. [*Aside*] Shall I hear more, or shall I speak at this?
    Jul. 'Tis but thy name that is my enemy.   40
Thou art thyself, though not a Montague.
What's Montague? It is nor hand, nor foot,
Nor arm, nor face, nor any other part
Belonging to a man. O, be some other name!
What's in a name? That which we call a rose   45
By any other name would smell as sweet.
So Romeo would, were he not Romeo called,

Cupid combating Death.
From Geoffrey Whitney, *Choice of Emblems* (1586).

48. **owes:** owns.
74. **let:** hindrance.
78. **proof:** protected (by armor).
81. **but thou love:** unless you love.

Retain that dear perfection which he owes
Without that title. Romeo, doff thy name;
And for that name, which is no part of thee,   50
Take all myself.

   Rom.   I take thee at thy word.
Call me but love, and I'll be new baptized;
Henceforth I never will be Romeo.

   Jul. What man art thou that, thus bescreened in night,   55
So stumblest on my counsel?

   Rom.   By a name
I know not how to tell thee who I am.
My name, dear saint, is hateful to myself,
Because it is an enemy to thee.   60
Had I it written, I would tear the word.

   Jul. My ears have yet not drunk a hundred words
Of that tongue's utterance, yet I know the sound.
Art thou not Romeo, and a Montague?

   Rom. Neither, fair saint, if either thee dislike.   65

   Jul. How camest thou hither, tell me, and wherefore?
The orchard walls are high and hard to climb,
And the place death, considering who thou art,
If any of my kinsmen find thee here.

   Rom. With love's light wings did I o'erperch these   70
      walls;
For stony limits cannot hold love out,
And what love can do, that dares love attempt.
Therefore thy kinsmen are no let to me.

   Jul. If they do see thee, they will murder thee.   75

   Rom. Alack, there lies more peril in thine eye
Than twenty of their swords! Look thou but sweet,
And I am proof against their enmity.

   Jul. I would not for the world they saw thee here.

   Rom. I have night's cloak to hide me from their sight;   80
And but thou love me, let them find me here.

83. **prorogued:** postponed.

93. **Fain:** gladly; **dwell on form:** linger over formal niceties.

94. **compliment:** formal politeness.

103. **fond:** doting.

104. **light:** unmaidenly; usually used in the stronger sense of "unchaste."

106. **strange:** distant.

111. **discovered:** uncovered, revealed.

My life were better ended by their hate
Than death prorogued, wanting of thy love.
 Jul. By whose direction foundst thou out this place?
 Rom. By love, that first did prompt me to enquire.   85
He lent me counsel, and I lent him eyes.
I am no pilot, yet, wert thou as far
As that vast shore washed with the farthest sea,
I would adventure for such merchandise.
 Jul. Thou knowest the mask of night is on my face;   90
Else would a maiden blush bepaint my cheek
For that which thou hast heard me speak tonight.
Fain would I dwell on form—fain, fain deny
What I have spoke; but farewell compliment!
Dost thou love me? I know thou wilt say "Ay";   95
And I will take thy word. Yet, if thou swearst,
Thou mayst prove false. At lovers' perjuries,
They say Jove laughs. O gentle Romeo,
If thou dost love, pronounce it faithfully.
Or if thou thinkst I am too quickly won,   100
I'll frown, and be perverse, and say thee nay,
So thou wilt woo; but else, not for the world.
In truth, fair Montague, I am too fond,
And therefore thou mayst think my 'havior light;
But trust me, gentleman, I'll prove more true   105
Than those that have more cunning to be strange.
I should have been more strange, I must confess,
But that thou overheardst, ere I was ware,
My true love's passion. Therefore pardon me,
And not impute this yielding to light love,   110
Which the dark night hath so discovered.
 Rom. Lady, by yonder blessed moon I swear,
That tips with silver all these fruit-tree tops—
 Jul. O, swear not by the moon, the inconstant moon,

125. **unadvised:** heedless, ill-considered.

That monthly changes in her circled orb, 115
Lest that thy love prove likewise variable.
  Rom. What shall I swear by?
  Jul.   Do not swear at all;
Or if thou wilt, swear by thy gracious self,
Which is the god of my idolatry, 120
And I'll believe thee.
  Rom.   If my heart's dear love—
  Jul. Well, do not swear. Although I joy in thee,
I have no joy of this contract tonight.
It is too rash, too unadvised, too sudden; 125
Too like the lightning, which doth cease to be
Ere one can say "It lightens." Sweet, good night!
This bud of love, by summer's ripening breath,
May prove a beauteous flow'r when next we meet.
Good night, good night! As sweet repose and rest 130
Come to thy heart as that within my breast!
  Rom. O, wilt thou leave me so unsatisfied?
  Jul. What satisfaction canst thou have tonight?
  Rom. The exchange of thy love's faithful vow for mine.
  Jul. I gave thee mine before thou didst request it; 135
And yet I would it were to give again.
  Rom. Wouldst thou withdraw it? For what purpose,
      love?
  Jul. But to be frank and give it thee again.
And yet I wish but for the thing I have. 140
My bounty is as boundless as the sea,
My love as deep; the more I give to thee,
The more I have, for both are infinite.
I hear some noise within. Dear love, adieu!
                     [*Nurse*] *calls within.*
Anon, good nurse! Sweet Montague, be true. 145
Stay but a little, I will come again.   [*Exit.*]

A falconer with a hooded bird.
From Antonio Doni, *L'academia Peregrina e i mondi* (1552).
(See also [III. ii.] 14.)

151. **thy bent of love:** the intention of your love.

153. **procure:** provide, arrange for.

161. **By-and-by:** at once.

170. **tassel-gentle:** male falcon.

171. **Bondage is hoarse and may not speak aloud:** that is, not being a free agent, I must be careful not to be overheard.

Rom. O blessed, blessed night! I am afeard,
Being in night, all this is but a dream,
Too flattering-sweet to be substantial.

[Re-enter *Juliet* above.]

Jul. Three words, dear Romeo, and good night indeed. 150
If that thy bent of love be honorable,
Thy purpose marriage, send me word tomorrow,
By one that I'll procure to come to thee,
Where and what time thou wilt perform the rite;
And all my fortunes at thy foot I'll lay   155
And follow thee my lord throughout the world.
  Nurse. (Within) Madam!
  Jul. I come, anon.—But if thou meanst not well,
I do beseech thee—
  Nurse. (Within) Madam!   160
  Jul.   By-and-by I come.—
To cease thy suit and leave me to my grief.
Tomorrow will I send.
  Rom.   So thrive my soul—
  Jul. A thousand times good night!   *Exit.* 165
  Rom. A thousand times the worse, to want thy light!
Love goes toward love as schoolboys from their books;
But love from love, towards school with heavy looks.

Enter *Juliet* again [, above].

  Jul. Hist! Romeo, hist! O for a falc'ner's voice
To lure this tassel-gentle back again!   170
Bondage is hoarse and may not speak aloud;
Else would I tear the cave where Echo lies,
And make her airy tongue more hoarse than mine

180. **My sweet:** this passage appears to have been variously garbled in the early texts. The First Quarto has "Madame," the Second Quarto and First Folio "My neece," the Third and Fourth Quartos "My dear." Our reading is from Folios Two, Three, and Four.

187. **still:** always; see I. i. 184 and 224.

192. **wanton:** heedless child.

194. **gyves:** bonds, fetters.

204. **ghostly father:** i.e., father confessor, as the next scene makes clear.

205. **dear hap:** great good fortune.

With repetition of my Romeo's name.
Romeo! 175

Rom. It is my soul that calls upon my name.
How silver-sweet sound lovers' tongues by night,
Like softest music to attending ears!

Jul. Romeo!

Rom. My sweet? 180

Jul. What o'clock tomorrow
Shall I send to thee?

Rom. By the hour of nine.

Jul. I will not fail. 'Tis twenty years till then.
I have forgot why I did call thee back. 185

Rom. Let me stand here till thou remember it.

Jul. I shall forget, to have thee still stand there,
Rememb'ring how I love thy company.

Rom. And I'll still stay, to have thee still forget,
Forgetting any other home but this. 190

Jul. 'Tis almost morning. I would have thee gone—
And yet no farther than a wanton's bird,
That lets it hop a little from her hand,
Like a poor prisoner in his twisted gyves,
And with a silk thread plucks it back again, 195
So loving-jealous of his liberty.

Rom. I would I were thy bird.

Jul. Sweet, so would I.
Yet I should kill thee with much cherishing.
Good night, good night! Parting is such sweet sorrow, 200
That I shall say good night till it be morrow. [*Exit.*]

Rom. Sleep dwell upon thine eyes, peace in thy breast!
Would I were sleep and peace, so sweet to rest!
Hence will I to my ghostly father's cell,
His help to crave and my dear hap to tell. 205

Exit.

[II. iii.] Romeo hastens from Juliet to the cell of their priest, Friar Laurence. He tells the Friar of his new love and asks him if he will marry them that very day. The Friar is troubled at the rapidity of Romeo's change of heart but agrees to perform the ceremony; he hopes that this marriage will bring about a peace between the two families.

llllllllllllllllllllllllllllllllll

5. **Titan:** the sun god, a child of Hyperion, one of the Titans. The name **Titan** was sometimes applied to the offspring of those gigantic beings.

8. **osier:** willow, wicker.

15. **None but for some:** i.e., no children (plants) but are good for some purpose.

16. **mickle:** great; **grace:** virtue; that is, effectiveness.

21. **Revolts from true birth:** i.e., denies its birthright.

26. **that part cheers each part:** its fragrance tones up every part of the body.

27. **with the heart:** as it stops the heart's action.

29. **grace:** divine grace, virtue; **will:** fleshly appetite, lust.

[Scene III. Friar Laurence's cell.]

Enter *Friar* [*Laurence*] alone, with a basket.

Friar. The grey-eyed morn smiles on the frowning
    night,
Chequ'ring the Eastern clouds with streaks of light;
And flecked darkness like a drunkard reels
From forth day's path and Titan's fiery wheels.   5
Now, ere the sun advance his burning eye
The day to cheer and night's dank dew to dry,
I must up-fill this osier cage of ours
With baleful weeds and precious-juiced flowers.
The earth that's nature's mother is her tomb,   10
What is her burying grave, that is her womb;
And from her womb children of divers kind
We sucking on her natural bosom find;
Many for many virtues excellent,
None but for some, and yet all different.   15
O, mickle is the powerful grace that lies
In plants, herbs, stones, and their true qualities;
For naught so vile that on the earth doth live
But to the earth some special good doth give;
Nor aught so good but, strained from that fair use,   20
Revolts from true birth, stumbling on abuse.
Virtue itself turns vice, being misapplied,
And vice sometime's by action dignified.
Within the infant rind of this small flower
Poison hath residence, and medicine power;   25
For this, being smelt, with that part cheers each part;
Being tasted, slays all senses with the heart.
Two such opposed kings encamp them still
In man as well as herbs—grace and rude will;

31. **canker:** cankerworm, devourer of flowers.

33. **Benedicite:** God bless you.

55. **physic:** medicine.

57. **My intercession likewise steads my foe:** my petition is on behalf of my enemy (Juliet) as well as myself.

58. **homely in thy drift:** that is, tell your story in plain English without quibbling.

59. **shrift:** absolution; see I. i. 160.

And where the worser is predominant, 30
Full soon the canker death eats up that plant.

Enter *Romeo*.

Rom. Good morrow, father.
Friar.   Benedicite!
What early tongue so sweet saluteth me?
Young son, it argues a distempered head 35
So soon to bid good morrow to thy bed.
Care keeps his watch in every old man's eye,
And where care lodges sleep will never lie;
But where unbruised youth with unstuffed brain
Doth couch his limbs, there golden sleep doth reign. 40
Therefore thy earliness doth me assure
Thou art uproused with some distemp'rature;
Or if not so, then here I hit it right—
Our Romeo hath not been in bed tonight.
Rom. That last is true, the sweeter rest was mine. 45
Friar. God pardon sin! Wast thou with Rosaline?
Rom. With Rosaline, my ghostly father? No.
I have forgot that name, and that name's woe.
Friar. That's my good son! But where hast thou been
    then? 50
Rom. I'll tell thee ere thou ask it me again.
I have been feasting with mine enemy,
Where on a sudden one hath wounded me
That's by me wounded. Both our remedies
Within thy help and holy physic lies. 55
I bear no hatred, blessed man, for, lo,
My intercession likewise steads my foe.
Friar. Be plain, good son, and homely in thy drift.
Riddling confession finds but riddling shrift.
Rom. Then plainly know my heart's dear love is set 60

63. **all combined:** i.e., Juliet and himself are united spiritually.

75. **season:** (1) salt; (2) preserve; **of it doth not taste:** does not seem to have been affected by it.

76. **thy sighs from heaven clears:** clears the air of his vaporous sighs with the heat of its rays.

82. **sentence:** maxim.

84. **chidst:** scolded.

93. **by rote:** from memory.

Tybert and Reynard the Fox.
From *The Most Delectable History of Reynard the Fox* (1694).
(See [II. iv.] 20.)

On the fair daughter of rich Capulet;
As mine on hers, so hers is set on mine,
And all combined, save what thou must combine
By holy marriage. When, and where, and how
We met, we wooed, and made exchange of vow,   65
I'll tell thee as we pass; but this I pray,
That thou consent to marry us today.

   Friar. Holy Saint Francis! What a change is here!
Is Rosaline, that thou didst love so dear,
So soon forsaken? Young men's love then lies   70
Not truly in their hearts, but in their eyes.
Jesu Maria! What a deal of brine
Hath washed thy sallow cheeks for Rosaline!
How much salt water thrown away in waste,
To season love, that of it doth not taste!   75
The sun not yet thy sighs from heaven clears,
Thy old groans ring yet in mine ancient ears.
Lo, here upon thy cheek the stain doth sit
Of an old tear that is not washed off yet.
If e'er thou wast thyself, and these woes thine,   80
Thou and these woes were all for Rosaline.
And art thou changed? Pronounce this sentence then:
Women may fall when there's no strength in men.

   Rom. Thou chidst me oft for loving Rosaline.
   Friar. For doting, not for loving, pupil mine.   85
   Rom. And badest me bury love.
   Friar.   Not in a grave
To lay one in, another out to have.
   Rom. I pray thee chide not. She whom I love now
Doth grace for grace and love for love allow.   90
The other did not so.
   Friar.   O, she knew well
Thy love did read by rote, that could not spell.
But come, young waverer, come go with me.

98. **stand:** insist.

||||||||||||||||||||||||||||||||||||||||||||||||||||

[**II. iv.**] Mercutio and Benvolio encounter Romeo in the street the next day and find him a changed man, his wit and good spirits restored. Juliet's nurse finds Romeo and he tells her of his plan to be married at Friar Laurence's cell that afternoon.

||||||||||||||||||||||||||||||||||||||

17. **butt-shaft:** practice arrow. Cupid, Mercutio implies, dispatched Romeo with his lightest ammunition.

20. **Prince of Cats:** a play on Tybalt's name, which corresponds closely with that of a Prince of Cats, Sir Tybert, in the beast epic of *Reynard the Fox*.

21. **compliments:** courteous formalities of the duel. The word was also a dueling term with the technical meaning "to respond to attack with the correct guard."

22. **pricksong:** written music; i.e., pricked out on a sheet. As **you sing pricksong** is therefore equivalent to "by the book," with a pun.

In one respect I'll thy assistant be;   95
For this alliance may so happy prove
To turn your households' rancor to pure love.
   Rom. O, let us hence! I stand on sudden haste.
   Friar. Wisely, and slow. They stumble that run fast.
                              Exeunt.

[Scene IV. A street.]

Enter *Benvolio* and *Mercutio*.

   Mer. Where the devil should this Romeo be?
Came he not home tonight?
   Ben. Not to his father's. I spoke with his man.
   Mer. Why, that same pale hard-hearted wench, that
     Rosaline,   5
Torments him so that he will sure run mad.
   Ben. Tybalt, the kinsman to old Capulet,
Hath sent a letter to his father's house.
   Mer. A challenge, on my life.
   Ben. Romeo will answer it.   10
   Mer. Any man that can write may answer a letter.
   Ben. Nay, he will answer the letter's master, how he
dares, being dared.
   Mer. Alas, poor Romeo, he is already dead! stabbed
with a white wench's black eye; shot through the ear   15
with a love song; the very pin of his heart cleft with the
blind bow-boy's butt-shaft; and is he a man to encounter
Tybalt?
   Ben. Why, what is Tybalt?
   Mer. More than Prince of Cats, I can tell you. O, he's   20
the courageous captain of compliments. He fights as you
sing pricksong—keeps time, distance, and proportion;

23. **minim rest:** a musical term for a short pause.

25. **of the very first house:** of the best fencing school; i.e., as expert a fencer as one can find.

26-7. **cause:** cause for dueling. Tybalt is quick to take offense; **passado:** (Italian *passata*) a step forward accompanied by a thrust; **punto reverso:** another Italian term: a backhanded thrust from the left side of the body; **hay:** *hai*, an exclamation of triumph at making a home thrust, probably from the Italian *ai*, "thou hast it."

29-30. **The pox of:** plague take; **antic:** grotesque; see I. [v.] 57; **fantasticoes:** affected persons; **new tuners of accent:** users of phrases currently in fashion.

31. **tall:** brave.

32. **grandsire:** a dig at Benvolio's dignity.

33. **flies:** parasites.

34. **form:** (1) fashion; (2) bench.

39. **numbers:** verses.

40. **Petrarch:** whose love sonnets to Laura were models for later sonnet writers.

42. **Dido:** the queen of Carthage, whose tragic love for Aeneas made her one of the famous lovers of the world; **Hero:** the beloved of Leander, who swam the Hellespont nightly to visit her until he was drowned in a storm.

43. **hildings:** worthless creatures; mere baggages; **Thisbe:** the beloved of Pyramus, whose love story is comically performed in *A Midsummer Night's Dream.*

45. **French slop:** full breeches cut in the French style.

49. **slip:** piece of counterfeit money; **conceive:** understand, get the point.

rests me his minim rest, one, two, and the third in your
bosom! the very butcher of a silk button, a duelist, a
duelist! a gentleman of the very first house, of the first   25
and second cause. Ah, the immortal *passado!* the *punto
reverso!* the *hay!*

Ben. The what?

Mer. The pox of such antic, lisping, affecting fantasticoes—these new tuners of accent! "By Jesu, a very good   30
blade! a very tall man! a very good whore!" Why, is not
this a lamentable thing, grandsire, that we should be thus
afflicted with these strange flies, these fashion-mongers,
these *pardona-mi's*, who stand so much on the new form
that they cannot sit at ease on the old bench? O, their   35
bones, their bones!

Enter *Romeo.*

Ben. Here comes Romeo! here comes Romeo!

Mer. Without his roe, like a dried herring. O flesh,
flesh, how art thou fishified! Now is he for the numbers
that Petrarch flowed in. Laura, to his lady, was but a   40
kitchen wench (marry, she had a better love to berhyme
her), Dido a dowdy, Cleopatra a gypsy, Helen and Hero
hildings and harlots, Thisbe a grey eye or so, but not to
the purpose. Signior Romeo, *bon jour!* There's a French
salutation to your French slop. You gave us the counter-   45
feit fairly last night.

Rom. Good morrow to you both. What counterfeit did
I give you?

Mer. The slip, sir, the slip. Can you not conceive?

Rom. Pardon, good Mercutio. My business was great,   50
and in such a case as mine a man may strain courtesy.

Mer. That's as much as to say, such a case as yours
constrains a man to bow in the hams.

60. **well-flowered: flowered** equals "pinked," i.e., decorated with a pattern of punched holes.

63-4. **solely singular:** the only sole (with a pun); emphatically alone.

65-6. **single-soled jest, solely singular for the singleness:** feeble, pathetic joke, unique for its weakness. *Single* was sometimes used in opposition to *double* in the sense of "lacking in strength."

68-9. **cry a match:** claim a triumph in the battle of wits.

72-3. **Was I with you there:** did I hit home; see "Am I come near ye now," I. [v.] 18.

78. **sweeting:** a variety of apple.

80-1. **a sweet goose:** i.e., Mercutio himself.

82. **of cheveril:** i.e., flexible.

85. **broad:** plain, evident to all beholders.

Rom. Meaning, to curtsy.

Mer. Thou hast most kindly hit it.   55

Rom. A most courteous exposition.

Mer. Nay, I am the very pink of courtesy.

Rom. Pink for flower.

Mer. Right.

Rom. Why, then is my pump well-flowered.   60

Mer. Well said! Follow me this jest now till thou hast
worn out thy pump, that, when the single sole of it is
worn, the jest may remain, after the wearing, solely
singular.

Rom. O single-soled jest, solely singular for the single- 65
ness!

Mer. Come between us, good Benvolio! My wits faint.

Rom. Switch and spurs, switch and spurs! or I'll cry a
match.

Mer. Nay, if our wits run the wild-goose chase, I am   70
done; for thou hast more of the wild goose in one of thy
wits than, I am sure, I have in my whole five. Was I with
you there for the goose?

Rom. Thou wast never with me for anything when
thou wast not there for the goose.   75

Mer. I will bite thee by the ear for that jest.

Rom. Nay, good goose, bite not!

Mer. Thy wit is a very bitter sweeting; it is a most
sharp sauce.

Rom. And is it not, then, well served in to a sweet   80
goose?

Mer. O, here's a wit of cheveril, that stretches from an
inch narrow to an ell broad!

Rom. I stretch it out for that word "broad," which,
added to the goose, proves thee far and wide a broad   85
goose.

Mer. Why, is not this better now than groaning for

90. **natural:** idiot.

99. **goodly gear:** handsome merchandise (facetious).

101. **smock:** the feminine equivalent of a shirt.

115. **By my troth:** truly.

Petrarch.
From *Il Petrarcha con l'espositione d'Alessandro Vellutello* (1538).

love? Now art thou sociable, now art thou Romeo; now
art thou what thou art, by art as well as by nature. For
this driveling love is like a great natural that runs lolling   90
up and down to hide his bauble in a hole.

Ben. Stop there, stop there!

Mer. Thou desirest me to stop in my tale against the
hair.

Ben. Thou wouldst else have made thy tale large.   95

Mer. O, thou art deceived! I would have made it short;
for I was come to the whole depth of my tale, and meant
indeed to occupy the argument no longer.

Enter *Nurse* and her *Man* [*Peter*].

Rom. Here's goodly gear!

Mer. A sail, a sail!   100

Ben. Two, two! a shirt and a smock.

Nurse. Peter!

Peter. Anon.

Nurse. My fan, Peter.

Mer. Good Peter, to hide her face; for her fan's the   105
fairer of the two.

Nurse. God ye good morrow, gentlemen.

Mer. God ye good-den, fair gentlewoman.

Nurse. Is it good-den?

Mer. 'Tis no less, I tell ye; for the bawdy hand of the   110
dial is now upon the prick of noon.

Nurse. Out upon you! What a man are you!

Rom. One, gentlewoman, that God hath made for himself to mar.

Nurse. By my troth, it is well said. "For himself to   115
mar," quoth 'a? Gentlemen, can any of you tell me where
I may find the young Romeo?

Rom. I can tell you; but young Romeo will be older

120. **fault:** lack.

122. **took:** understood.

126. **endite:** Benvolio is using a pretentious word for invite.

127. **So ho:** a cry used by hunters on sighting game.

129. **lenten:** i.e., made during Lent.

130. **something:** somewhat.

140-41. **lady, lady, lady:** probably a line from a well-known ballad.

143. **merchant:** chap, which derives from "chapman" (merchant); possibly also with a pun on "merchant ship"; **ropery:** knavery; an adjective used to describe actions which ought to lead to the gallows.

when you have found him than he was when you sought
him. I am the youngest of that name, for fault of a worse. 120

Nurse. You say well.

Mer. Yea, is the worst well? Very well took, i' faith!
wisely, wisely.

Nurse. If you be he, sir, I desire some confidence with
you. 125

Ben. She will endite him to some supper.

Mer. A bawd, a bawd, a bawd! So ho!

Rom. What hast thou found?

Mer. No hare, sir; unless a hare, sir, in a lenten pie,
that is something stale and hoar ere it be spent. 130

He walks by them and sings.

An old hare hoar,
And an old hare hoar,
Is very good meat in Lent;
But a hare that is hoar
Is too much for a score 135
When it hoars ere it be spent.

Romeo, will you come to your father's? We'll to dinner
thither.

Rom. I will follow you.

Mer. Farewell, ancient lady. Farewell, [*sings*] lady, 140
lady, lady. *Exeunt Mercutio, Benvolio.*

Nurse. Marry, farewell! I pray you, sir, what saucy
merchant was this that was so full of his ropery?

Rom. A gentleman, nurse, that loves to hear himself
talk and will speak more in a minute than he will stand 145
to in a month.

Nurse. An 'a speak anything against me, I'll take him
down, an 'a were lustier than he is, and twenty such

149. **Jacks:** knaves, rascals; **Scurvy:** contemptible.

150. **flirt-gills:** light wenches.

150-51. **skains-mates:** fellow cutthroats. A skain was a kind of knife much in use in the underworld of the time.

162. **were:** would be.

166. **commend me:** give my respectful greetings.

171. **mark:** take note of; listen to.

179. **Go to:** say no more; see I. [v.] 81.

A dueling stance.
From Angelo Vizani, *Trattato dello schermo* (1588).

Jacks; and if I cannot, I'll find those that shall. Scurvy
knave! I am none of his flirt-gills; I am none of his skains-   150
mates. And thou must stand by too, and suffer every
knave to use me at his pleasure!

Peter. I saw no man use you at his pleasure. If I had,
my weapon should quickly have been out, I warrant you.
I dare draw as soon as another man, if I see occasion in   155
a good quarrel, and the law on my side.

Nurse. Now, afore God, I am so vexed that every part
about me quivers. Scurvy knave! Pray you, sir, a word;
and, as I told you, my young lady bid me enquire you out.
What she bid me say, I will keep to myself; but first let   160
me tell ye, if ye should lead her into a fool's paradise, as
they say, it were a very gross kind of behavior, as they
say; for the gentlewoman is young; and therefore, if you
should deal double with her, truly it were an ill thing to
be offered to any gentlewoman, and very weak dealing.   165

Rom. Nurse, commend me to thy lady and mistress. I
protest unto thee—

Nurse. Good heart, and i' faith I will tell her as much.
Lord, Lord! she will be a joyful woman.

Rom. What wilt thou tell her, nurse? Thou dost not   170
mark me.

Nurse. I will tell her, sir, that you do protest, which,
as I take it, is a gentlemanlike offer.

Rom. Bid her devise
Some means to come to shrift this afternoon;   175
And there she shall at Friar Laurence' cell
Be shrived and married. Here is for thy pains.

Nurse. No, truly, sir; not a penny.

Rom. Go to! I say you shall.

Nurse. This afternoon, sir? Well, she shall be there.   180

Rom. And stay, good nurse, behind the abbey wall.
Within this hour my man shall be with thee

183. **tackled stair:** rope ladder.

184. **topgallant:** pinnacle. The **topgallant** was the highest section of a ship's mast.

186. **quit:** reward.

191. **Two may keep counsel, putting one away:** proverbial: Three may keep counsel if two away.

195. **would fain:** is eager to; see [II. ii.] 93.

195-96. **lay knife aboard:** take for himself what he wants, like a pirate; **lief:** willingly; **a very:** an actual.

198. **properer:** more handsome.

199. **clout:** rag; **versal world:** i.e., the universe.

200. **a letter:** that is, the same letter.

202. **that's the dog's name:** because it sounds like a dog snarling.

204. **sententious:** a comic mistake for *sententiae* (sentences, sayings); see [II. iii.] 82; **of you and rosemary: rosemary** symbolized remembrance, as Shakespeare makes plain in *Hamlet*, IV. [v.] 190. Juliet, according to the Nurse, has been composing pretty speeches on the theme of her eternal remembrance of her lover Romeo.

209. **apace:** quickly.

And bring thee cords made like a tackled stair,
Which to the high topgallant of my joy
Must be my convoy in the secret night.   185
Farewell. Be trusty, and I'll quit thy pains.
Farewell. Commend me to thy mistress.

   Nurse. Now God in heaven bless thee! Hark you, sir.
   Rom. What sayst thou, my dear nurse?
   Nurse. Is your man secret? Did you ne'er hear say,   190
Two may keep counsel, putting one away?
   Rom. I warrant thee my man's as true as steel.
   Nurse. Well, sir, my mistress is the sweetest lady.
Lord, Lord! when 'twas a little prating thing—O, there is
a nobleman in town, one Paris, that would fain lay knife 195
aboard; but she, good soul, had as lief see a toad, a very
toad, as see him. I anger her sometimes, and tell her that
Paris is the properer man; but I'll warrant you, when I
say so, she looks as pale as any clout in the versal world.
Doth not rosemary and Romeo begin both with a letter? 200
   Rom. Ay, nurse, what of that? Both with an R.
   Nurse. Ah, mocker! that's the dog's name. R is for
the—No; I know it begins with some other letter; and she
hath the prettiest sententious of it, of you and rosemary,
that it would do you good to hear it.   205
   Rom. Commend me to thy lady.
   Nurse. Ay, a thousand times. [*Exit Romeo.*] Peter!
   Peter. Anon.
   Nurse. Peter, take my fan, and go before, and apace.
                                  Exeunt.

[II. v.] Juliet waits impatiently for the return of her nurse with word from Romeo. The news is finally pried from the garrulous old woman. Juliet is to give out that she has gone to confession at Friar Laurence's cell, and there she and Romeo will be married.

▬▬▬▬▬▬▬▬▬▬▬▬▬▬

6. **lowering:** darkening.

7. **nimble-pinioned:** fast-winged, swift; **Love:** i.e., the goddess of love.

12. **affections:** emotional capacity.

14. **bandy:** toss.

16. **feign:** appear; **as:** as if.

23. **news:** often used in a plural form, since the original meaning of the word was "new things."

[Scene V. Capulet's orchard.]

Enter *Juliet*.

Jul. The clock struck nine when I did send the nurse;
In half an hour she promised to return.
Perchance she cannot meet him. That's not so.
O, she is lame! Love's heralds should be thoughts,
Which ten times faster glide than the sun's beams   5
Driving back shadows over lowering hills.
Therefore do nimble-pinioned doves draw Love,
And therefore hath the wind-swift Cupid wings.
Now is the sun upon the highmost hill
Of this day's journey, and from nine till twelve   10
Is three long hours; yet she is not come.
Had she affections and warm youthful blood,
She would be as swift in motion as a ball;
My words would bandy her to my sweet love,
And his to me.   15
But old folks, many feign as they were dead—
Unwieldy, slow, heavy and pale as lead.

Enter *Nurse* [and *Peter*].

O God, she comes! O honey nurse, what news?
Hast thou met with him? Send thy man away.
  Nurse. Peter, stay at the gate.   20
                           [*Exit Peter.*]
  Jul. Now, good sweet nurse—O Lord, why lookst thou
    sad?
Though news be sad, yet tell them merrily;
If good, thou shamest the music of sweet news
By playing it to me with so sour a face.   25

26. **give me leave:** excuse me (while I catch my breath).

27. **jaunce:** rough journey.

37. **stay the circumstance:** wait to hear the whole story.

38. **satisfied:** informed.

52. **Beshrew:** "curse," though used casually.

56. **honest:** honorable; see [II. i.] 30.

Nurse. I am aweary, give me leave awhile.
Fie, how my bones ache! What a jaunce have I had!

Jul. I would thou hadst my bones, and I thy news.
Nay, come, I pray thee speak. Good, good nurse, speak.

Nurse. Jesu, what haste! Can you not stay awhile? 30
Do you not see that I am out of breath?

Jul. How art thou out of breath when thou hast breath
To say to me that thou art out of breath?
The excuse that thou dost make in this delay
Is longer than the tale thou dost excuse. 35
Is thy news good or bad? Answer to that.
Say either, and I'll stay the circumstance.
Let me be satisfied, is't good or bad?

Nurse. Well, you have made a simple choice; you
know not how to choose a man. Romeo? No, not he. 40
Though his face be better than any man's, yet his leg
excels all men's; and for a hand and a foot, and a body,
though they be not to be talked on, yet they are past
compare. He is not the flower of courtesy, but, I'll warrant him, as gentle as a lamb. Go thy ways, wench; serve 45
God. What, have you dined at home?

Jul. No, no. But all this did I know before.
What says he of our marriage? What of that?

Nurse. Lord, how my head aches! What a head have I!
It beats as it would fall in twenty pieces. 50
My back o' t' other side—ah, my back, my back!
Beshrew your heart for sending me about
To catch my death with jauncing up and down!

Jul. I' faith, I am sorry that thou art not well.
Sweet, sweet, sweet nurse, tell me, what says my love? 55

Nurse. Your love says, like an honest gentleman, and a
courteous, and a kind, and a handsome, and, I warrant, a
virtuous—Where is your mother?

Jul. Where is my mother? Why, she is within.

64. **Marry come up:** "really, contain yourself, give me a chance to get my breath"; **trow:** declare; see I. [iii.] 37.

67. **coil:** to-do.

━━━━━━━━━━━━━━━━━━

[**II. vi.**] Romeo and Juliet meet at Friar Laurence's cell.

━━━━━━━━━━━

4. **countervail:** outweigh.

Where should she be? How oddly thou repliest! 60
"Your love says, like an honest gentleman,
'Where is your mother?'"
    Nurse.   O God's Lady dear!
Are you so hot? Marry come up, I trow.
Is this the poultice for my aching bones? 65
Henceforward do your messages yourself.
    Jul. Here's such a coil! Come, what says Romeo?
    Nurse. Have you got leave to go to shrift today?
    Jul. I have.
    Nurse. Then hie you hence to Friar Laurence' cell; 70
There stays a husband to make you a wife.
Now comes the wanton blood up in your cheeks:
They'll be in scarlet straight at any news.
Hie you to church; I must another way,
To fetch a ladder, by the which your love 75
Must climb a bird's nest soon when it is dark.
I am the drudge, and toil in your delight;
But you shall bear the burden soon at night.
Go; I'll to dinner; hie you to the cell.
    Jul. Hie to high fortune! Honest nurse, farewell. 80
                         Exeunt.

[Scene VI. Friar Laurence's cell.]

Enter *Friar* [*Laurence*] and *Romeo.*

    Friar. So smile the heavens upon this holy act
That after-hours with sorrow chide us not!
    Rom. Amen, amen! But come what sorrow can,
It cannot countervail the exchange of joy
That one short minute gives me in her sight.
Do thou but close our hands with holy words, 5
Then love-devouring death do what he dare—

12. **Is loathsome in his own deliciousness:** i.e., quickly becomes offensive by its excess of sweetness.

13. **confounds:** destroys.

18. **gossamer:** cobweb.

20. **vanity:** that is, the hollow pursuit of mortal delights.

23. **As much:** that is, the same greeting.

25. **that:** if.

26. **blazon:** proclaim.

30. **Conceit:** understanding; see **conceive**, [II. iv.] 49.

It is enough I may but call her mine.
    Friar. These violent delights have violent ends
And in their triumph die, like fire and powder,   10
Which, as they kiss, consume. The sweetest honey
Is loathsome in his own deliciousness
And in the taste confounds the appetite.
Therefore love moderately: long love doth so;
Too swift arrives as tardy as too slow.   15

Enter Juliet.

Here comes the lady. O, so light a foot
Will ne'er wear out the everlasting flint.
A lover may bestride the gossamer
That idles in the wanton summer air,
And yet not fall; so light is vanity.   20
    Jul. Good even to my ghostly confessor.
    Friar. Romeo shall thank thee, daughter, for us both.
    Jul. As much to him, else is his thanks too much.
    Rom. Ah, Juliet, if the measure of thy joy
Be heaped like mine, and that thy skill be more   25
To blazon it, then sweeten with thy breath
This neighbor air, and let rich music's tongue
Unfold the imagined happiness that both
Receive in either by this dear encounter.
    Jul. Conceit, more rich in matter than in words,   30
Brags of his substance, not of ornament.
They are but beggars that can count their worth;
But my true love is grown to such excess
I cannot sum up sum of half my wealth.
    Friar. Come, come with me, and we will make short   35
        work;
For, by your leaves, you shall not stay alone
Till Holy Church incorporate two in one.
[Exeunt.]

THE TRAGEDY OF

ROMEO AND JULIET

ACT III

[III. i.] Mercutio and Benvolio meet Tybalt on the street. When Romeo appears Tybalt deliberately insults him, but Romeo gives him soft answers. Mercutio is incensed and challenges Tybalt; they duel and Mercutio is given a death wound under Romeo's arm as he attempts to separate them. Ashamed at what may appear his weakness, since his new relationship to Juliet and Tybalt is secret, Romeo engages with Tybalt and kills him. When the Capulets learn of Tybalt's death they demand Romeo's life in exchange, in accordance with the Prince's previous threat. They discount Benvolio's report of the order of events. The Prince orders Romeo's banishment on pain of death.

▪▪▪▪▪▪▪▪▪▪▪▪▪▪▪▪▪▪▪▪▪▪▪▪

8. **by the operation of the second cup:** as the second drink stirs his senses.

9. **drawer:** dispenser of drink, waiter.

12. **moved to be moody:** inclined to temper.

13. **moody to be moved:** angry at being crossed.

15. **two:** Mercutio pretends to misunderstand Benvolio's **to.**

[ACT III]

[Scene I. A public place.]

Enter *Mercutio, Benvolio,* and *Men.*

Ben. I pray thee, good Mercutio, let's retire.
The day is hot, the Capulets abroad,
And if we meet, we shall not scape a brawl,
For now, these hot days, is the mad blood stirring.

Mer. Thou art like one of these fellows that, when he   5
enters the confines of a tavern, claps me his sword upon
the table and says "God send me no need of thee!" and
by the operation of the second cup draws him on the
drawer, when indeed there is no need.

Ben. Am I like such a fellow?   10

Mer. Come, come, thou art as hot a Jack in thy mood
as any in Italy; and as soon moved to be moody, and as
soon moody to be moved.

Ben. And what to?

Mer. Nay, an there were two such, we should have   15
none shortly, for one would kill the other. Thou! why,
thou wilt quarrel with a man that hath a hair more or a
hair less in his beard than thou hast. Thou wilt quarrel
with a man for cracking nuts, having no other reason but
because thou hast hazel eyes. What eye but such an eye   20
would spy out such a quarrel? Thy head is as full of quarrels as an egg is full of meat; and yet thy head hath been

49

27. **doublet:** a snug-fitting male jacket.

28. **riband:** ribbon.

31. **fee simple:** unconditional ownership. In legal terms, a **fee simple** is an inheritance which is passed on to the heirs without any restricting limitations.

31-2. **an hour and a quarter:** that is, a fraction of its actual value.

44. **Consort:** a term used for a company of musicians.

47. **Zounds:** God's wounds.

The insult.
From Achille Marozzo, *Arte dell' armi* (1568).

beaten as addle as an egg for quarreling. Thou hast quar-
reled with a man for coughing in the street, because he
hath wakened thy dog that hath lain asleep in the sun.   25
Didst thou not fall out with a tailor for wearing his new
doublet before Easter? with another for tying his new
shoes with old riband? And yet thou wilt tutor me from
quarreling!

Ben. An I were so apt to quarrel as thou art, any man   30
should buy the fee simple of my life for an hour and a
quarter.

Mer. The fee simple? O simple!

Enter *Tybalt* and others.

Ben. By my head, here come the Capulets.
Mer. By my heel, I care not.   35
Tyb. Follow me close, for I will speak to them.
Gentlemen, good den. A word with one of you.
Mer. And but one word with one of us?
Couple it with something; make it a word and a blow.
Tyb. You shall find me apt enough to that, sir, an you   40
will give me occasion.
Mer. Could you not take some occasion without giving?
Tyb. Mercutio, thou consortest with Romeo.
Mer. Consort? What, dost thou make us minstrels? An
thou make minstrels of us, look to hear nothing but dis-   45
cords. Here's my fiddlestick; here's that shall make you
dance. Zounds, consort!
Ben. We talk here in the public haunt of men.
Either withdraw unto some private place
And reason coldly of your grievances,   50
Or else depart. Here all eyes gaze on us.
· *Mer.* Men's eyes were made to look, and let them gaze.
I will not budge for no man's pleasure, I.

56. **livery:** uniform; see [II. ii.] 8. Mercutio is offended at Tybalt's speaking of Romeo as though he were his servant.

57. **go before to field, he'll be your follower:** that is, he'll be quick to follow you to the field of honor if you provoke him, but in no other sense can he be called your **follower** (retainer).

60. **a villain:** i.e., one of low birth; not a knave as in modern usage.

62. **appertaining:** suitable.

70. **tender:** cherish.

73. **Alla stoccata carries it away: alla stoccata** was a fencing term meaning "at the thrust." Mercutio uses the term to mean Tybalt because of the direct way he has shown his hostility to Romeo verbally, in contrast to Romeo's courteous replies.

74. **ratcatcher:** i.e., cat; **will you walk:** an invitation to duel.

77. **make bold withal:** assault; i.e., he hopes to take one life.

77-8. **and, as you shall use me hereafter, dry-beat the rest of the eight:** that is, depending on whether the loss of one of your lives softens your manner, I may only thrash the rest of your eight lives.

79. **pilcher:** Mercutio combines "pilch," a leather garment, "pilcher," an abusive term for a thief, and probably "pilcher/pilchard," a small fish akin to the herring, to refer to Tybalt's scabbard in as offensive a way as he can think of; **ears:** hilts; commonly used in a plural form.

83. **passado:** see [II. iv.] 26.

Enter *Romeo*.

Tyb. Well, peace be with you, sir. Here comes my
  man.   55

Mer. But I'll be hanged, sir, if he wear your livery.
Marry, go before to field, he'll be your follower!
Your worship in that sense may call him man.

Tyb. Romeo, the love I bear thee can afford
No better term than this: thou art a villain.   60

Rom. Tybalt, the reason that I have to love thee
Doth much excuse the appertaining rage
To such a greeting. Villain am I none.
Therefore farewell. I see thou knowst me not.

Tyb. Boy, this shall not excuse the injuries   65
That thou hast done me; therefore turn and draw.

Rom. I do protest I never injured thee,
But love thee better than thou canst devise
Till thou shalt know the reason of my love;
And so, good Capulet, which name I tender   70
As dearly as mine own, be satisfied.

Mer. O calm, dishonorable, vile submission!
Alla stoccata carries it away.   [*Draws.*]
Tybalt, you ratcatcher, will you walk?

Tyb. What wouldst thou have with me?   75

Mer. Good King of Cats, nothing but one of your nine
lives. That I mean to make bold withal, and, as you shall
use me hereafter, dry-beat the rest of the eight. Will you
pluck your sword out of his pilcher by the ears? Make
haste, lest mine be about your ears ere it be out.   80

Tyb. I am for you.   [*Draws.*]

Rom. Gentle Mercutio, put thy rapier up.

Mer. Come, sir, your *passado!*   [*They fight.*]

Rom. Draw, Benvolio; beat down their weapons.

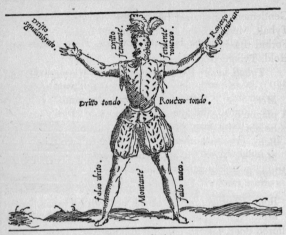

A fencing diagram.
From Achille Marozzo, *Arte dell' armi* (1568).

85. **forbear:** give over, forgo.

87. **Verona streets:** the use of proper nouns, without possessive endings, to act as adjectives, was common.

90. **sped:** undone, destroyed.

98-9. **peppered:** completely finished.

101-2. **by the book of arithmetic:** by one of the Italian or French treatises on fencing, complete with diagrams.

109. **ally:** relative.

110. **very:** unquestioned, faithful.

Gentlemen, for shame! forbear this outrage! 85
Tybalt, Mercutio, the Prince expressly hath
Forbid this bandying in Verona streets.
Hold, Tybalt! Good Mercutio!

*Tybalt under Romeo's arm thrusts Mercutio in, and
flies [with his Men].*

Mer.   I am hurt.
A plague o' both your houses! I am sped. 90
Is he gone and hath nothing?

Ben.   What, art thou hurt?

Mer. Ay, ay, a scratch, a scratch. Marry, 'tis enough.
Where is my page? Go, villain, fetch a surgeon.

[Exit Page.]

Rom. Courage, man. The hurt cannot be much. 95

Mer. No, 'tis not so deep as a well, nor so wide as a
church door; but 'tis enough, 'twill serve. Ask for me tomorrow, and you shall find me a grave man. I am peppered, I warrant, for this world. A plague o' both your
houses! Zounds, a dog, a rat, a mouse, a cat, to scratch a 100
man to death! A braggart, a rogue, a villain, that fights by
the book of arithmetic! Why the devil came you between
us? I was hurt under your arm.

Rom. I thought all for the best.

Mer. Help me into some house, Benvolio, 105
Or I shall faint. A plague o' both your houses!
They have made worms' meat of me. I have it,
And soundly too. Your houses!

Exit [supported by Benvolio].

Rom. This gentleman, the Prince's near ally,
My very friend, hath got this mortal hurt
In my behalf—my reputation stained 110
With Tybalt's slander—Tybalt, that an hour
Hath been my kinsman. O sweet Juliet,

Dueling steps.

From Henri de Saint Didier, *Traicte contenant les secrets du premier livre sur l'espee seule* (1573; 1907 reprint).

116. **brave:** noble.

117. **aspired:** attained or soared to.

119. **mo:** more; **depend:** impend, cast a threatening shadow over.

123. **respective:** thoughtful, considerate; **lenity:** lenience, mercy.

135. **amazed:** dumbstruck; **doom thee:** sentence thee to.

137. **fool:** i.e., plaything.

Thy beauty hath made me effeminate
And in my temper softened valor's steel!   115

Enter *Benvolio*.

Ben. O Romeo, Romeo, brave Mercutio's dead!
That gallant spirit hath aspired the clouds,
Which too untimely here did scorn the earth.
Rom. This day's black fate on mo days doth depend;
This but begins the woe others must end.   120

Enter *Tybalt*.

Ben. Here comes the furious Tybalt back again.
Rom. Alive in triumph, and Mercutio slain?
Away to heaven respective lenity,
And fire-eyed fury be my conduct now!
Now, Tybalt, take the "villain" back again   125
That late thou gavest me, for Mercutio's soul
Is but a little way above our heads,
Staying for thine to keep him company.
Either thou or I, or both, must go with him.
Tyb. Thou, wretched boy, that didst consort him here,   130
Shalt with him hence.
Rom.   This shall determine that.
                        They fight. Tybalt falls.
Ben. Romeo, away, be gone!
The citizens are up, and Tybalt slain.
Stand not amazed. The Prince will doom thee death   135
If thou art taken. Hence, be gone, away!
Rom. O, I am fortune's fool!
Ben.   Why dost thou stay?
                        Exit Romeo.

The beginning of a duel.

From Henri de Saint Didier, *Traicte contenant les secrets du premier livre sur l'espee seule* (1573; 1907 reprint).

145. **discover:** reveal; see [II. ii.] 111.
146. **manage:** conduct.
157. **nice:** trifling.

Enter Citizens.

Citizen. Which way ran he that killed Mercutio?
Tybalt, that murderer, which way ran he?   140
    Ben. There lies that Tybalt.
    Citizen.   Up, sir, go with me.
I charge thee in the Prince's name obey.

Enter Prince [with his Train], Old Montague, Capulet,
    their Wives, and [others].

    Prince. Where are the vile beginners of this fray?
    Ben. O noble Prince, I can discover all   145
The unlucky manage of this fatal brawl.
There lies the man, slain by young Romeo,
That slew thy kinsman, brave Mercutio.
    Cap. Wife. Tybalt, my cousin! O my brother's child!
O Prince! O cousin! O husband! O, the blood is spilled 150
Of my dear kinsman! Prince, as thou art true,
For blood of ours shed blood of Montague.
O cousin, cousin!
    Prince. Benvolio, who began this bloody fray?
    Ben. Tybalt, here slain, whom Romeo's hand did slay. 155
Romeo, that spoke him fair, bid him bethink
How nice the quarrel was, and urged withal
Your high displeasure. All this—uttered
With gentle breath, calm look, knees humbly bowed—
Could not take truce with the unruly spleen   160
Of Tybalt deaf to peace, but that he tilts
With piercing steel at bold Mercutio's breast;
Who, all as hot, turns deadly point to point,
And, with a martial scorn, with one hand beats
Cold death aside and with the other sends   165

167. **Retorts:** returns.
171. **envious:** malicious; see I. i. 152.
172. **stout:** valiant.
174. **entertained:** given thought to.
180. **Affection:** partiality.
193. **My blood:** i.e., that of his own kin.
194. **amerce:** punish.
195. **mine:** i.e., my blood.
197. **purchase out:** buy immunity for.

Phaëton.
From Geoffrey Whitney, *Choice of Emblems* (1586).
(See [III. ii.] 3.)

It back to Tybalt, whose dexterity
Retorts it. Romeo he cries aloud,
"Hold, friends! friends, part!" and swifter than his tongue,
His agile arm beats down their fatal points,
And 'twixt them rushes; underneath whose arm   170
An envious thrust from Tybalt hit the life
Of stout Mercutio, and then Tybalt fled,
But by-and-by comes back to Romeo,
Who had but newly entertained revenge,
And to't they go like lightning; for, ere I   175
Could draw to part them, was stout Tybalt slain;
And, as he fell, did Romeo turn and fly.
This is the truth, or let Benvolio die.

   Cap. Wife. He is a kinsman to the Montague;
Affection makes him false, he speaks not true.   180
Some twenty of them fought in this black strife,
And all those twenty could but kill one life.
I beg for justice, which thou, Prince, must give.
Romeo slew Tybalt; Romeo must not live.

   Prince. Romeo slew him; he slew Mercutio.   185
Who now the price of his dear blood doth owe?

   Mon. Not Romeo, Prince; he was Mercutio's friend;
His fault concludes but what the law should end,
The life of Tybalt.

   Prince.   And for that offense   190
Immediately we do exile him hence.
I have an interest in your hate's proceeding,
My blood for your rude brawls doth lie a-bleeding;
But I'll amerce you with so strong a fine
That you shall all repent the loss of mine.   195
I will be deaf to pleading and excuses;
Nor tears nor prayers shall purchase out abuses.
Therefore use none. Let Romeo hence in haste,

[III. ii.] Juliet, awaiting her husband, is told by the Nurse of Tybalt's death at Romeo's hand. She is grief-stricken for her cousin but tries to take some comfort in the fact that Tybalt wished to kill Romeo. Romeo is banished but the Nurse promises to bring him secretly to Juliet's chamber before he leaves Verona.

2. **Phoebus:** the sun god.

3. **Phaëton:** the son of Phoebus, who lacked experience in driving the chariot of the sun and could not control the horses.

6. **runaways' eyes:** the eyes of unwanted observers. This expression has caused endless controversy as to its meaning. The Variorum edition of the play contains twenty-nine pages on whether the meaning ought to be "runaway eyes," "runaway's eyes," or "runaways' eyes," since the early texts do not agree; **wink:** close and thus fail to see.

10. **civil:** courteous.

12. **learn:** used as a transitive verb in the sixteenth century, as it is still a transitive verb in unsophisticated speech today, to mean the equivalent of "teach."

14. **Hood:** conceal; **unmanned:** untamed; **bating:** fluttering in revolt. The passage is from falconry. A falcon was said to "bate" when it became excited and fluttered its wings, and it was quieted by placing a hood over its head.

Else, when he is found, that hour is his last.
Bear hence this body, and attend our will.   200
Mercy but murders, pardoning those that kill.

Exeunt.

[Scene II. Capulet's orchard.]

Enter *Juliet* alone.

Jul. Gallop apace, you fiery-footed steeds,
Towards Phoebus' lodging! Such a wagoner
As Phaëton would whip you to the West
And bring in cloudy night immediately.
Spread thy close curtain, love-performing night,   5
That runaways' eyes may wink, and Romeo
Leap to these arms untalked of and unseen.
Lovers can see to do their amorous rites
By their own beauties; or, if love be blind,
It best agrees with night. Come, civil night,   10
Thou sober-suited matron, all in black,
And learn me how to lose a winning match,
Played for a pair of stainless maidenhoods.
Hood my unmanned blood, bating in my cheeks,
With thy black mantle; till strange love, grown bold,   15
Think true love acted simple modesty.
Come, night; come, Romeo; come, thou day in night;
For thou wilt lie upon the wings of night
Whiter than new snow upon a raven's back.
Come, gentle night; come, loving, black-browed night;   20
Give me my Romeo; and, when he shall die,
Take him and cut him out in little stars,
And he will make the face of heaven so fine
That all the world will be in love with night

A cockatrice.

From Horapollo, *De sacris notis et sculpturis* (1551).

S.D. after l. 31. **Enter Nurse . . .** : from First Quarto. The Nurse presumably entered and sank to a seat and, with the cords in her lap, began wringing her hands.

39. **well-a-day:** alas.

48. **"I":** ay (yes), usually so spelled in Elizabethan days.

50. **cockatrice:** a fabulous creature which could kill with one glance of its eyes; also sometimes confused with the basilisk.

And pay no worship to the garish sun.   25
O, I have bought the mansion of a love,
But not possessed it; and though I am sold,
Not yet enjoyed. So tedious is this day
As is the night before some festival
To an impatient child that hath new robes   30
And may not wear them. O, here comes my nurse,

Enter Nurse, *wringing her hands, with the ladder
of cords in her lap.*

And she brings news; and every tongue that speaks
But Romeo's name speaks heavenly eloquence.
Now, nurse, what news? What hast thou there? the cords
That Romeo bid thee fetch?   35
  Nurse.   Ay, ay, the cords.
  Jul. Ay me! what news? Why dost thou wring thy
    hands?
  Nurse. Ah, well-a-day! he's dead, he's dead, he's dead!
We are undone, lady, we are undone!   40
Alack the day! he's gone, he's killed, he's dead!
  Jul. Can heaven be so envious?
  Nurse.   Romeo can,
Though heaven cannot. O Romeo, Romeo!
Who ever would have thought it? Romeo!   45
  Jul. What devil art thou that dost torment me thus?
This torture should be roared in dismal hell.
Hath Romeo slain himself? Say thou but "I,"
And that bare vowel "I" shall poison more
Than the death-darting eye of cockatrice.   50
I am not I, if there be such an "I";
Or those eyes shut that make thee answer "I."
If he be slain, say "I"; or if not, "no."
Brief sounds determine of my weal or woe.

56. **God save the mark:** a phrase uttered to deflect the bad luck which might result from seeing or mentioning a disastrous thing.

57. **corse:** corpse.

59. **swounded:** swooned.

60. **bankrout:** bankrupt.

62. **Vile earth, to earth resign:** wretched body, resign yourself to death.

72. **banished:** pronounced as three syllables here and in the other lines where it is so spelled.

77. **keep:** protect, guard.

78. **tyrant:** usurper, the usual sense of the word in reference to ancient historical rulers. The series of phrases which follow all describe the deceitful usurpation of mild and innocent beauty by creatures of opposite characteristics.

81. **justly:** rightly.

Nurse. I saw the wound, I saw it with mine eyes,   55
(God save the mark!) here on his manly breast.
A piteous corse, a bloody piteous corse;
Pale, pale as ashes, all bedaubed in blood,
All in gore blood. I swounded at the sight.

Jul. O, break, my heart! poor bankrout, break at once!   60
To prison, eyes; ne'er look on liberty!
Vile earth, to earth resign; end motion here,
And thou and Romeo press one heavy bier!

Nurse. O Tybalt, Tybalt, the best friend I had!
O courteous Tybalt! honest gentleman!   65
That ever I should live to see thee dead!

Jul. What storm is this that blows so contrary?
Is Romeo slaughtered, and is Tybalt dead?
My dear-loved cousin, and my dearer lord?
Then, dreadful trumpet, sound the general doom!   70
For who is living, if those two are gone?

Nurse. Tybalt is gone, and Romeo banished;
Romeo that killed him, he is banished.

Jul. O God! Did Romeo's hand shed Tybalt's blood?

Nurse. It did, it did! alas the day, it did!   75

Jul. O serpent heart, hid with a flow'ring face!
Did ever dragon keep so fair a cave?
Beautiful tyrant! fiend angelical!
Dove-feathered raven! wolvish-ravening lamb!
Despised substance of divinest show!   80
Just opposite to what thou justly seemst—
A damned saint, an honorable villain!
O nature, what hadst thou to do in hell
When thou didst bower the spirit of a fiend
In mortal paradise of such sweet flesh?   85
Was ever book containing such vile matter
So fairly bound? O, that deceit should dwell
In such a gorgeous palace!

91. **forsworn:** oath-breaking, faithless; **naught:** wicked; **dissemblers:** deceivers.

92. **aqua vitae:** spirits, probably brandy.

115. **fain:** gladly, eagerly; see [II. iv.] 195.

Nurse.   There's no trust,
No faith, no honesty in men; all perjured,   90
All forsworn, all naught, all dissemblers.
Ah, where's my man? Give me some aqua vitae.
These griefs, these woes, these sorrows make me old.
Shame come to Romeo!
  Jul.   Blistered be thy tongue   95
For such a wish! He was not born to shame.
Upon his brow shame is ashamed to sit;
For 'tis a throne where honor may be crowned
Sole monarch of the universal earth.
O, what a beast was I to chide at him!   100
  Nurse. Will you speak well of him that killed your
   cousin?
  Jul. Shall I speak ill of him that is my husband?
Ah, poor my lord, what tongue shall smooth thy name
When I, thy three-hours' wife, have mangled it?   105
But wherefore, villain, didst thou kill my cousin?
That villain cousin would have killed my husband.
Back, foolish tears, back to your native spring!
Your tributary drops belong to woe,
Which you, mistaking, offer up to joy.   110
My husband lives, that Tybalt would have slain;
And Tybalt's dead, that would have slain my husband.
All this is comfort; wherefore weep I then?
Some word there was, worser than Tybalt's death,
That murdered me. I would forget it fain;   115
But O, it presses to my memory
Like damned guilty deeds to sinners' minds!
"Tybalt is dead, and Romeo—banished."
That "banished," that one word "banished,"
Hath slain ten thousand Tybalts. Tybalt's death   120
Was woe enough, if it had ended there;
Or, if sour woe delights in fellowship

126. **modern:** ordinary.

127. **rearward:** company bringing up the rear, the opposite of vanguard.

135. **bring:** escort.

146. **wot:** know.

Mourning for Tybalt.
From Tommaso Porcacchi, *Funerali antichi* (1574).

And needly will be ranked with other griefs,
Why followed not, when she said "Tybalt's dead,"
Thy father, or thy mother, nay, or both,   125
Which modern lamentation might have moved?
But with a rearward following Tybalt's death,
"Romeo is banished"—to speak that word
Is father, mother, Tybalt, Romeo, Juliet,
All slain, all dead. "Romeo is banished"—   130
There is no end, no limit, measure, bound,
In that word's death; no words can that woe sound.
Where is my father and my mother, nurse?
　　Nurse. Weeping and wailing over Tybalt's corse.
Will you go to them? I will bring you thither.   135
　　Jul. Wash they his wounds with tears? Mine shall be
　　　spent,
When theirs are dry, for Romeo's banishment.
Take up those cords. Poor ropes, you are beguiled,
Both you and I, for Romeo is exiled.   140
He made you for a highway to my bed;
But I, a maid, die maiden-widowed.
Come, cords; come, nurse. I'll to my wedding bed;
And death, not Romeo, take my maidenhead!
　　Nurse. Hie to your chamber. I'll find Romeo   145
To comfort you. I wot well where he is.
Hark ye, your Romeo will be here at night.
I'll to him; he is hid at Laurence' cell.
　　Jul. O, find him! give this ring to my true knight
And bid him come to take his last farewell.   150

　　　　　　　　　　　　　　　　　　Exeunt.

[III. iii.] Friar Laurence reports to Romeo that the Prince has ordered him banished instead of executed, but Romeo despairs at the thought of separation from Juliet. The Nurse enters and bids him hasten to Juliet and comfort her. Friar Laurence sends Romeo to Juliet, with the hope that in time he may be pardoned and permitted to return to Verona. In the meantime he will live in Mantua, and Friar Laurence will convey news to him through his man Balthasar.

━━━━━━━━━━━━━━

18. **patient:** calm, unmoved.
19. **Verona walls:** see [III. i.] 87.
22. **world's exile:** i.e., exile from the world.

[Scene III. Friar Laurence's cell.]

Enter *Friar* [*Laurence*].

Friar. Romeo, come forth; come forth, thou fearful man.
Affliction is enamored of thy parts,
And thou art wedded to calamity.

Enter *Romeo*.

Rom. Father, what news? What is the Prince's doom?   5
What sorrow craves acquaintance at my hand
That I yet know not?
    Friar.   Too familiar
Is my dear son with such sour company.
I bring thee tidings of the Prince's doom.   10
    Rom. What less than doomsday is the Prince's doom?
    Friar. A gentler judgment vanished from his lips—
Not body's death, but body's banishment.
    Rom. Ha, banishment? Be merciful, say "death";
For exile hath more terror in his look,   15
Much more than death. Do not say "banishment."
    Friar. Hence from Verona art thou banished.
Be patient, for the world is broad and wide.
    Rom. There is no world without Verona walls,
But purgatory, torture, hell itself.   20
Hence banished is banist from the world,
And world's exile is death. Then "banishment"
Is death mistermed. Calling death "banishment,"
Thou cuttst my head off with a golden axe
And smilest upon the stroke that murders me.   25
    Friar. O deadly sin! O rude unthankfulness!

28. **rushed:** pushed.

30. **dear:** i.e., extraordinary in kind. **Dear** is often used to intensify the meaning of the noun which it modifies.

35. **validity:** worth.

36. **courtship:** gallant attentions and the privileges of a courtier may both be meant.

54. **fond:** foolish.

Thy fault our law calls death; but the kind Prince,
Taking thy part, hath rushed aside the law,
And turned that black word death to banishment.
This is dear mercy, and thou seest it not.　　　　30
　　Rom. 'Tis torture, and not mercy. Heaven is here,
Where Juliet lives; and every cat and dog
And little mouse, every unworthy thing,
Live here in heaven and may look on her;
But Romeo may not. More validity,　　　　35
More honorable state, more courtship lives
In carrion flies than Romeo. They may seize
On the white wonder of dear Juliet's hand
And steal immortal blessing from her lips,
Who, even in pure and vestal modesty,　　　　40
Still blush, as thinking their own kisses sin;
But Romeo may not—he is banished.
This may flies do, when I from this must fly;
They are free men, but I am banished.
And sayst thou yet that exile is not death?　　　　45
Hadst thou no poison mixed, no sharp-ground knife,
No sudden mean of death, though ne'er so mean,
But "banished" to kill me—"banished"?
O friar, the damned use that word in hell;
Howling attends it! How hast thou the heart,　　　　50
Being a divine, a ghostly confessor,
A sin-absolver, and my friend professed,
To mangle me with that word "banished"?
　　Friar. Thou fond mad man, hear me a little speak.
　　Rom. O, thou wilt speak again of banishment.　　　　55
　　Friar. I'll give thee armor to keep off that word;
Adversity's sweet milk, philosophy,
To comfort thee, though thou art banished.
　　Rom. Yet "banished"? Hang up philosophy!
Unless philosophy can make a Juliet,　　　　60

64. **when that:** when.

66. **dispute:** discuss; **estate:** condition, state of luck.

Displant a town, reverse a prince's doom,
It helps not, it prevails not. Talk no more.

   Friar. O, then I see that madmen have no ears.

   Rom. How should they, when that wise men have no
     eyes? 65

   Friar. Let me dispute with thee of thy estate.

   Rom. Thou canst not speak of that thou dost not feel.
Wert thou as young as I, Juliet thy love,
An hour but married, Tybalt murdered,
Doting like me, and like me banished, 70
Then mightst thou speak, then mightst thou tear thy hair,
And fall upon the ground, as I do now,
Taking the measure of an unmade grave.

                    Nurse knocks [within].

   Friar. Arise; one knocks. Good Romeo, hide thyself.

   Rom. Not I; unless the breath of heartsick groans 75
Mist-like infold me from the search of eyes. *Knock.*

   Friar. Hark, how they knock! Who's there? Romeo,
     arise;
Thou wilt be taken.—Stay awhile!—Stand up; *Knock.*
Run to my study.—By-and-by!—God's will, 80
What simpleness is this.—I come, I come! *Knock.*
Who knocks so hard? Whence come you? What's your
     will?

   Nurse. [*Within*] Let me come in, and you shall know
     my errand. 85
I come from Lady Juliet.

   Friar.   Welcome then.

               Enter *Nurse.*

   Nurse. O holy friar, O, tell me, holy friar,
Where is my lady's lord, where's Romeo?

92. **even:** exactly, just.

93. **woeful sympathy:** sorrowful agreement.

98. **O:** expression of grief.

102. **old:** that is, a murderer of unusual callousness. **Old** is still used as an intensive in provincial Southern speech.

112. **level:** aim.

123. **ill-beseeming:** inappropriate; see I. [v.] 77. That is, it is improper behavior in an animal to take on the appearance of humanity and to fail to simulate properly either a man or a woman.

Friar. There on the ground, with his own tears made   90
    drunk.
Nurse. O, he is even in my mistress' case,
Just in her case! O woeful sympathy!
Piteous predicament! Even so lies she,
Blubb'ring and weeping, weeping and blubbering.   95
Stand up, stand up! Stand, an you be a man.
For Juliet's sake, for her sake, rise and stand!
Why should you fall into so deep an O?
  Rom. (*Rises*) Nurse—
  Nurse. Ah sir! ah sir! Well, death's the end of all.   100
  Rom. Spakest thou of Juliet? How is it with her?
Doth not she think me an old murderer,
Now I have stained the childhood of our joy
With blood removed but little from her own?
Where is she? and how doth she? and what says   105
My concealed lady to our canceled love?
  Nurse. O, she says nothing, sir, but weeps and weeps;
And now falls on her bed, and then starts up,
And Tybalt calls; and then on Romeo cries,
And then down falls again.   110
  Rom.   As if that name,
Shot from the deadly level of a gun,
Did murder her; as that name's cursed hand
Murdered her kinsman. O tell me, friar, tell me,
In what vile part of this anatomy
Doth my name lodge? Tell me, that I may sack   115
The hateful mansion.   [*Draws his dagger.*]
  Friar.   Hold thy desperate hand.
Art thou a man? Thy form cries out thou art;
Thy tears are womanish, thy wild acts denote
The unreasonable fury of a beast.   120
Unseemly woman in a seeming man!
Or ill-beseeming beast in seeming both!

129. **railst . . . on:** complain against.

133. **usurer:** moneylender.

134. **use:** a pun on the usual meaning and the meaning "lend at interest."

Thou hast amazed me. By my holy order,
I thought thy disposition better tempered.   125
Hast thou slain Tybalt? Wilt thou slay thyself?
And slay thy lady too that lives in thee,
By doing damned hate upon thyself?
Why railst thou on thy birth, the heaven, and earth?
Since birth and heaven and earth, all three do meet   130
In thee at once; which thou at once wouldst lose.
Fie, fie, thou shamest thy shape, thy love, thy wit,
Which, like a usurer, aboundst in all,
And usest none in that true use indeed
Which should bedeck thy shape, thy love, thy wit.   135
Thy noble shape is but a form of wax,
Digressing from the valor of a man;
Thy dear love sworn but hollow perjury,
Killing that love which thou hast vowed to cherish;
Thy wit, that ornament to shape and love,   140
Misshapen in the conduct of them both,
Like powder in a skilless soldier's flask,
Is set afire by thine own ignorance,
And thou dismembered with thine own defense.
What, rouse thee, man! Thy Juliet is alive,   145
For whose dear sake thou wast but lately dead.
There art thou happy. Tybalt would kill thee,
But thou slewest Tybalt. There art thou happy.
The law, that threatened death, becomes thy friend
And turns it to exile. There art thou happy.   150
A pack of blessings light upon thy back;
Happiness courts thee in her best array;
But, like a misbehaved and sullen wench,
Thou poutst upon thy fortune and thy love.
Take heed, take heed, for such die miserable.   155
Go get thee to thy love, as was decreed,
Ascend her chamber, hence and comfort her.

158. **the watch be set:** the night watch takes up its post at the gates of Verona.

161. **blaze:** blazon, announce; see [II. vi.] 26; **your friends:** both your families.

167. **apt:** inclined.

175. **comfort:** happiness.

176-77. **here stands all your state:** this is your whole situation.

But look thou stay not till the watch be set,
For then thou canst not pass to Mantua,
Where thou shalt live till we can find a time   160
To blaze your marriage, reconcile your friends,
Beg pardon of the Prince, and call thee back
With twenty hundred thousand times more joy
Than thou wentst forth in lamentation.
Go before, nurse. Commend me to thy lady,   165
And bid her hasten all the house to bed,
Which heavy sorrow makes them apt unto.
Romeo is coming.

Nurse. O Lord, I could have stayed here all the night
To hear good counsel. O, what learning is!   170
My lord, I'll tell my lady you will come.

Rom. Do so, and bid my sweet prepare to chide.

Nurse offers to go and turns again.

Nurse. Here is a ring she bid me give you, sir.
Hie you, make haste, for it grows very late.   *Exit.*

Rom. How well my comfort is revived by this!   175

Friar. Go hence; good night; and here stands all your
state:
Either be gone before the watch be set,
Or by the break of day disguised from hence.
Sojourn in Mantua. I'll find out your man,   180
And he shall signify from time to time
Every good hap to you that chances here.
Give me thy hand. 'Tis late. Farewell; good night.

Rom. But that a joy past joy calls out on me,
It were a grief so brief to part with thee.   185
Farewell.

Exeunt.

[III. iv.] Paris and Capulet again discuss Paris' suit. In the desperate hope that marriage will make Juliet forget her sorrow for Tybalt, Capulet consents that Paris marry Juliet in three days.

||||||||||||||||||||||||||||||

1. **fall'n out:** happened.
2. **move:** influence (on your behalf).
11. **mewed up to:** confined with. Trained falcons, maintained for hunting, were kept in buildings called "mews"; **heaviness:** grief; see "heavy," I. i. 138 and I. [iv.] 12.
12. **desperate:** rash; **tender:** offer.
21. **A:** on.
24. **ado:** ceremony.
25. **late:** recently.
26. **held him carelessly:** had little regard for him.

[Scene IV. Capulet's house.]

Enter *Old Capulet,* his *Wife,* and *Paris.*

Cap. Things have fall'n out, sir, so unluckily
That we have had no time to move our daughter.
Look you, she loved her kinsman Tybalt dearly,
And so did I. Well, we were born to die.
'Tis very late; she'll not come down tonight.   5
I promise you, but for your company,
I would have been abed an hour ago.

Par. These times of woe afford no time to woo.
Madam, good night. Commend me to your daughter.

Lady. I will, and know her mind early tomorrow;   10
Tonight she's mewed up to her heaviness.

   Paris offers to go and Capulet calls him again.

Cap. Sir Paris, I will make a desperate tender
Of my child's love. I think she will be ruled
In all respects by me; nay more, I doubt it not.
Wife, go you to her ere you go to bed;   15
Acquaint her here of my son Paris' love
And bid her (mark you me?) on Wednesday next—
But, soft! what day is this?

Par.   Monday, my lord.

Cap. Monday! ha, ha! Well, Wednesday is too soon.   20
A Thursday let it be—a Thursday, tell her,
She shall be married to this noble earl.
Will you be ready? Do you like this haste?
We'll keep no great ado—a friend or two;
For hark you, Tybalt being slain so late,   25
It may be thought we held him carelessly,
Being our kinsman, if we revel much.

33. **against:** for, usually "in preparation for."
35. **Afore me:** my word; a casual oath.

━━━━━━━━━━━━━━━━━━━━━━━━━━━━

[III. v.] Romeo and Juliet say farewell at day-break. He is no sooner gone than her mother enters to tell Juliet of her forthcoming marriage to Paris. Juliet is horrified. When she attempts to dissuade her parents, they are infuriated at her disobedience and her father threatens to disown her if she will not consent to the honorable match they have arranged. Her nurse gives her the worldly advice that Paris is a better match than banished Romeo. Juliet pretends to be persuaded but secretly decides that the Nurse shall know no more of her affairs and that she must rely on Friar Laurence's help.

━━━━━━━━━━━━━━━━━━━

8. **lace:** streak; **severing:** scattering.
9. **Night's candles:** i.e., the stars.
13. **meteor:** the flash of a meteor through the sky was then thought to be a stream of fiery gas from one of the heavenly bodies.

Therefore we'll have some half a dozen friends,
And there an end. But what say you to Thursday?

Par. My lord, I would that Thursday were tomorrow.   30

Cap. Well, get you gone. A Thursday be it then.
Go you to Juliet ere you go to bed;
Prepare her, wife, against this wedding day.
Farewell, my lord.—Light to my chamber, ho!
Afore me, it is so very very late   35
That we may call it early by-and-by.
Good night.

                                   Exeunt.

[Scene V. Capulet's orchard.]

Enter *Romeo* and *Juliet* aloft, at the window.

Jul. Wilt thou be gone? It is not yet near day.
It was the nightingale, and not the lark,
That pierced the fearful hollow of thine ear.
Nightly she sings on yond pomegranate tree.
Believe me, love, it was the nightingale.   5

Rom It was the lark, the herald of the morn;
No nightingale Look, love, what envious streaks
Do lace the severing clouds in yonder East.
Night's candles are burnt out, and jocund day
Stands tiptoe on the misty mountain tops.   10
I must be gone and live, or stay and die.

Jul. Yond light is not daylight; I know it, I.
It is some meteor that the sun exhales
To be to thee this night a torchbearer
And light thee on thy way to Mantua.   15
Therefore stay yet; thou needst not to be gone.

Rom. Let me be ta'en, let me be put to death.

Diana.

From Richard Whitcombe, *Janua divorum* (1678).

19. **yon grey is not the morning's eye:** the beginning light in the dark sky is not caused by the sun.

20. **reflex:** reflection; **Cynthia's brow:** Cynthia is one name for the goddess of the moon (Diana). She was sometimes pictured with a crescent moon on her forehead.

22. **vaulty:** vaulted.

23. **care:** eagerness.

29. **division:** a musical term for a melodic phrase.

31. **changed eyes:** i.e., because the ugly toad's large and brilliant eyes would be more appropriate to the lark.

33. **affray:** frighten. Afraid is the past participle.

34. **hunt's-up:** an early morning song to arouse hunters.

44. **friend:** lover.

I am content, so thou wilt have it so.
I'll say yon grey is not the morning's eye,
'Tis but the pale reflex of Cynthia's brow;   20
Nor that is not the lark whose notes do beat
The vaulty heaven so high above our heads.
I have more care to stay than will to go.
Come, death, and welcome! Juliet wills it so.
How is't, my soul? Let's talk; it is not day.   25

Jul. It is, it is! Hie hence, be gone, away!
It is the lark that sings so out of tune,
Straining harsh discords and unpleasing sharps.
Some say the lark makes sweet division;
This doth not so, for she divideth us.   30
Some say the lark and loathed toad changed eyes;
O, now I would they had changed voices too,
Since arm from arm that voice doth us affray,
Hunting thee hence with hunt's-up to the day!
O, now be gone! More light and light it grows.   35

Rom. More light and light—more dark and dark our
woes!

Enter *Nurse*, hastily.

Nurse. Madam!
Jul. Nurse?
Nurse. Your lady mother is coming to your chamber.   40
The day is broke; be wary, look about.   [*Exit.*]
Jul. Then, window, let day in, and let life out.
Rom. Farewell, farewell! One kiss, and I'll descend.
                                        He goeth down.
Jul. Art thou gone so, my lord, my love, my friend?
I must hear from thee every day in the hour,   45
For in a minute there are many days.

47. **much in years:** greatly aged.

55. **ill-divining:** i.e., foreseeing evil.

60. **Dry sorrow drinks our blood:** sorrow is pictured as thirsty because it was the popular belief of the time that it dissipated the body fluids, the blood in particular.

63. **renowmed:** renowned.

69. **procures:** brings.

O, by this count I shall be much in years
Ere I again behold my Romeo!
  Rom. Farewell!
I will omit no opportunity   50
That may convey my greetings, love, to thee.
  Jul. O, thinkst thou we shall ever meet again?
  Rom. I doubt it not; and all these woes shall serve
For sweet discourses in our time to come.
  Jul. O God, I have an ill-divining soul!   55
Methinks I see thee, now thou art below,
As one dead in the bottom of a tomb.
Either my eyesight fails, or thou lookst pale.
  Rom. And trust me, love, in my eye so do you.
Dry sorrow drinks our blood. Adieu! adieu!   *Exit.*   60
  Jul. O Fortune, Fortune! all men call thee fickle.
If thou art fickle, what dost thou with him
That is renowmed for faith? Be fickle, Fortune,
For then I hope thou wilt not keep him long
But send him back.   65
  Lady. [*Within*] Ho, daughter! are you up?
  Jul. Who is't that calls? It is my lady mother.
Is she not down so late, or up so early?
What unaccustomed cause procures her hither?

Enter *Mother*.

  Lady. Why, how now, Juliet?   70
  Jul.   Madam, I am not well.
  Lady. Evermore weeping for your cousin's death?
What, wilt thou wash him from his grave with tears?
An if thou couldst, thou couldst not make him live.
Therefore have done. Some grief shows much of love;   75
But much of grief shows still some want of wit.

77. **feeling:** deeply felt.

94. **runagate:** runaway.

99. **dead:** Juliet is choosing her words very carefully in order to say what will seem appropriate to her mother without really attacking Romeo.

102. **temper:** i.e., adulterate, though her mother will assume she means to mix in other deadly ingredients.

Jul. Yet let me weep for such a feeling loss.

Lady. So shall you feel the loss, but not the friend
Which you weep for.

Jul.   Feeling so the loss,   80
I cannot choose but ever weep the friend.

Lady. Well, girl, thou weepst not so much for his death
As that the villain lives which slaughtered him.

Jul. What villain, madam?

Lady.   That same villain Romeo.   85

Jul. [*Aside*] Villain and he be many miles asunder.—
God pardon him! I do, with all my heart;
And yet no man like he doth grieve my heart.

Lady. That is because the traitor murderer lives.

Jul. Ay, madam, from the reach of these my hands.   90
Would none but I might venge my cousin's death!

Lady. We will have vengeance for it, fear thou not.
Then weep no more. I'll send to one in Mantua,
Where that same banished runagate doth live,
Shall give him such an unaccustomed dram   95
That he shall soon keep Tybalt company;
And then I hope thou wilt be satisfied.

Jul. Indeed I never shall be satisfied
With Romeo till I behold him—dead—
Is my poor heart so for a kinsman vexed.   100
Madam, if you could find out but a man
To bear a poison, I would temper it;
That Romeo should, upon receipt thereof,
Soon sleep in quiet. O, how my heart abhors
To hear him named and cannot come to him,   105
To wreak the love I bore my cousin Tybalt
Upon his body that hath slaughtered him!

Lady. Find thou the means, and I'll find such a man.
But now I'll tell thee joyful tidings, girl.

112. **careful:** i.e., full of care for your well-being.

114. **sorted out:** selected.

116. **in happy time:** opportunely; see I. i. 159 and 238.

134. **conduit:** fountain.

Jul. And joy comes well in such a needy time.   110
What are they. I beseech your ladyship?

Lady. Well, well, thou hast a careful father, child;
One who, to put thee from thy heaviness,
Hath sorted out a sudden day of joy
That thou expects not nor I looked not for.   115

Jul. Madam, in happy time! What day is that?

Lady. Marry, my child. early next Thursday morn
The gallant, young. and noble gentleman,
The County Paris. at Saint Peter's Church,
Shall happily make thee there a joyful bride.   120

Jul. Now by Saint Peter's Church, and Peter too,
He shall not make me there a joyful bride!
I wonder at this haste. that I must wed
Ere he that should be husband comes to woo.
I pray you tell my lord and father, madam,   125
I will not marry yet; and when I do, I swear
It shall be Romeo, whom you know I hate,
Rather than Paris. These are news indeed!

Lady. Here comes your father. Tell him so yourself,
And see how he will take it at your hands.   130

Enter *Capulet* and *Nurse*.

Cap. When the sun sets the air doth drizzle dew,
But for the sunset of my brother's son
It rains downright.
How now? a conduit, girl? What, still in tears?
Evermore show'ring? In one little body   135
Thou counterfeitst a bark, a sea, a wind:
For still thy eyes, which I may call the sea,
Do ebb and flow with tears; the bark thy body is,
Sailing in this salt flood; the winds, thy sighs,
Who, raging with thy tears and they with them,   140

146. **take me with you:** i.e., let me understand you.

149. **wrought:** arranged for.

154. **choplogic:** quibbler.

156. **minion:** darling, with the implication of being spoiled.

158. **fettle:** prepare.

160. **a hurdle:** a wooden frame or sledge on which criminals were transported to their place of execution.

161. **green-sickness carrion: green-sickness** is a kind of anemia which affects young girls. Capulet is saying in effect, "you pale and sickly piece of flesh."

163. **Fie, fie:** she addresses her husband, dismayed at the violence of his anger.

165. **but to:** just long enough to.

170. **itch:** that is, to hit you.

Without a sudden calm will overset
Thy tempest-tossed body. How now, wife?
Have you delivered to her our decree?

Lady. Ay, sir; but she will none, she gives you thanks.
I would the fool were married to her grave! 145

Cap. Soft! take me with you, take me with you, wife.
How? Will she none? Doth she not give us thanks?
Is she not proud? Doth she not count her blest,
Unworthy as she is, that we have wrought
So worthy a gentleman to be her bridegroom? 150

Jul. Not proud you have, but thankful that you have.
Proud can I never be of what I hate,
But thankful even for hate that is meant love.

Cap. How, how, how, how, choplogic? What is this?
"Proud"—and "I thank you"—and "I thank you not"— 155
And yet "not proud"? Mistress minion you,
Thank me no thankings, nor proud me no prouds,
But fettle your fine joints 'gainst Thursday next
To go with Paris to Saint Peter's Church,
Or I will drag thee on a hurdle thither. 160
Out, you green-sickness carrion! out, you baggage!
You tallow-face!

Lady.   Fie, fie; what, are you mad?

Jul. Good father, I beseech you on my knees,
                    She kneels down.
Hear me with patience but to speak a word. 165

Cap. Hang thee, young baggage! disobedient wretch!
I tell thee what—get thee to church a Thursday
Or never after look me in the face.
Speak not, reply not, do not answer me!
My fingers itch. Wife, we scarce thought us blest 170
That God had lent us but this only child;
But now I see this one is one too much,

174. **hilding:** wretch; see [II. iv.] 43.

176. **rate:** berate, scold.

178. **Smatter:** chatter, babble of things you know nothing about.

183. **gossip's bowl:** a hot punch.

186. **God's bread:** an oath on the wafer representing the body of Christ in the Holy Communion.

193. **parts:** characteristics.

195. **puling:** whining.

196. **mammet:** doll; **in her fortunes tender:** i.e., inexperienced.

199. **pardon you:** i.e., excuse you from this company, be glad to see the last of you.

201. **I do not use to:** that is, it is not my habit.

202. **advise:** take careful thought.

And that we have a curse in having her.
Out on her, hilding!

Nurse.   God in heaven bless her!   175
You are to blame, my lord, to rate her so.

Cap. And why, my Lady Wisdom? Hold your tongue,
Good Prudence. Smatter with your gossips, go!

Nurse. I speak no treason.

Cap.   O, God-i-god-en!   180

Nurse. May not one speak?

Cap.   Peace, you mumbling fool!
Utter your gravity o'er a gossip's bowl,
For here we need it not.

Lady.   You are too hot.   185

Cap. God's bread! it makes me mad. Day, night, late,
          early,
At home, abroad, alone, in company,
Waking or sleeping, still my care hath been
To have her matched; and having now provided   190
A gentleman of princely parentage,
Of fair demesnes, youthful, and nobly trained,
Stuffed, as they say, with honorable parts,
Proportioned as one's thought would wish a man—
And then to have a wretched puling fool,   195
A whining mammet, in her fortunes tender,
To answer "I'll not wed, I cannot love;
I am too young, I pray you pardon me"!
But, an you will not wed, I'll pardon you.
Graze where you will, you shall not house with me.   200
Look to't, think on't; I do not use to jest.
Thursday is near; lay hand on heart, advise:
An you be mine, I'll give you to my friend;
An you be not, hang, beg, starve, die in the streets,
For, by my soul, I'll ne'er acknowledge thee,   205

207. **Trust to't:** be assured of it.

221-22. **practice stratagems/ Upon:** attempt to trap.

226. **all the world to nothing:** i.e., the odds are all to nothing.

227. **challenge:** claim.

232. **to:** compared with.

233. **quick:** lively, animated.

234. **Beshrew:** confound; see [II. v.] 52.

238. **here:** on earth.

Nor what is mine shall never do thee good.
Trust to't. Bethink you. I'll not be forsworn.   *Exit.*

    Jul. Is there no pity sitting in the clouds
That sees into the bottom of my grief?
O sweet my mother, cast me not away!   210
Delay this marriage for a month, a week;
Or if you do not, make the bridal bed
In that dim monument where Tybalt lies.

    Lady. Talk not to me, for I'll not speak a word.
Do as thou wilt, for I have done with thee.   *Exit.* 215

    Jul. O God!—O nurse, how shall this be prevented?
My husband is on earth, my faith in heaven.
How shall that faith return again to earth
Unless that husband send it me from heaven
By leaving earth? Comfort me, counsel me.   220
Alack, alack, that heaven should practice stratagems
Upon so soft a subject as myself!
What sayst thou? Hast thou not a word of joy?
Some comfort, nurse.

    Nurse.   Faith, here it is.   225
Romeo is banisht; and all the world to nothing
That he dares ne'er come back to challenge you;
Or if he do, it needs must be by stealth.
Then, since the case so stands as now it doth,
I think it best you married with the County.   230
O, he's a lovely gentleman!
Romeo's a dishclout to him. An eagle, madam,
Hath not so green, so quick, so fair an eye
As Paris hath. Beshrew my very heart,
I think you are happy in this second match,   235
For it excels your first; or if it did not,
Your first is dead—or 'twere as good he were
As living here and you no use of him.

    Jul. Speakst thou this from thy heart?

248. **Ancient damnation:** you old devil.

249. **forsworn:** i.e., guilty of breaking her vow of marriage to Romeo.

253. **bosom:** confidence.

Nurse. And from my soul too; else beshrew them both.   240
Jul. Amen!
Nurse. What?
Jul. Well, thou hast comforted me marvelous much.
Go in; and tell my lady I am gone,
Having displeased my father, to Laurence' cell,   245
To make confession and to be absolved.
   Nurse. Marry, I will; and this is wisely done.   *Exit.*
   Jul. Ancient damnation! O most wicked fiend!
Is it more sin to wish me thus forsworn,
Or to dispraise my lord with that same tongue   250
Which she hath praised him with above compare
So many thousand times? Go, counselor!
Thou and my bosom henceforth shall be twain.
I'll to the friar to know his remedy.
If all else fail, myself have power to die.   255
                              Exit.

THE TRAGEDY OF

ROMEO AND JULIET

ACT IV

[IV. i.] Paris is arranging with Friar Laurence for his wedding to Juliet when she arrives. After Paris leaves, the Friar gives Juliet a drug to take the night before her wedding. The drug will produce the effect of death; she will be placed in the family burial vault; and the Friar and Romeo will be there to spirit her from Verona when she awakens.

━━━━━━━━━━━━━━━━━━

3. **nothing slow to slack his haste:** not at all reluctant, which might slow him down.

5. **Uneven:** difficult.

10. **That she do give her sorrow so much sway:** that she allows her grief to overpower her.

13. **alone:** i.e., solitary.

[ACT IV]

[Scene I. Friar Laurence's cell.]

Enter *Friar* [*Laurence*] and *County Paris*.

Friar. On Thursday, sir? The time is very short.
Par. My father Capulet will have it so,
And I am nothing slow to slack his haste.
Friar. You say you do not know the lady's mind.
Uneven is the course; I like it not.   5
Par. Immoderately she weeps for Tybalt's death,
And therefore have I little talked of love;
For Venus smiles not in a house of tears.
Now, sir, her father counts it dangerous
That she do give her sorrow so much sway,   10
And in his wisdom hastes our marriage
To stop the inundation of her tears,
Which, too much minded by herself alone,
May be put from her by society.
Now do you know the reason of this haste.   15
Friar. [*Aside*] I would I knew not why it should be
      slowed.—
Look, sir, here comes the lady toward my cell.

Enter *Juliet.*

Par. Happily met, my lady and my wife!
Jul. That may be, sir, when I may be a wife.   20

77

42. **entreat:** beg; i.e., ask you to leave us.

43. **shield:** prevent.

49. **compass:** limit; **strains me past the compass of my wits:** stretches my wisdom past its limits.

50. **prorogue:** postpone; see [II. ii.] 83.

Par. That may be must be, love, on Thursday next.
Jul. What must be shall be.
Friar.   That's a certain text.
Par. Come you to make confession to this father?
Jul. To answer that, I should confess to you.   25
Par. Do not deny to him that you love me.
Jul. I will confess to you that I love him.
Par. So will ye, I am sure, that you love me.
Jul. If I do so, it will be of more price,
Being spoke behind your back, than to your face.   30
Par. Poor soul, thy face is much abused with tears.
Jul. The tears have got small victory by that,
For it was bad enough before their spite.
Par. Thou wrongst it more than tears with that report.
Jul. That is no slander, sir, which is a truth;   35
And what I spake, I spake it to my face.
Par. Thy face is mine, and thou hast slandered it.
Jul. It may be so, for it is not mine own.
Are you at leisure, holy father, now,
Or shall I come to you at evening mass?   40
Friar. My leisure serves me, pensive daughter, now.
My lord, we must entreat the time alone.
Par. God shield I should disturb devotion!
Juliet, on Thursday early will I rouse ye.
Till then, adieu, and keep this holy kiss.   *Exit.*   45
Jul. O, shut the door! and when thou hast done so,
Come weep with me—past hope, past cure, past help!
Friar. Ah, Juliet, I already know thy grief;
It strains me past the compass of my wits.
I hear thou must, and nothing may prorogue it,   50
On Thursday next be married to this County.
Jul. Tell me not, friar, that thou hearst of this,
Unless thou tell me how I may prevent it.
If in thy wisdom thou canst give no help,

59. **deed:** a legal document, proof of ownership.

66. **the commission of thy years and art:** that is, your years and art acting together as an authoritative body.

77. **copest:** deals, tries to bargain.

81. **thievish ways:** in roads where thieves lurk.

83. **charnel house:** storehouse for bones uncovered in digging new graves.

85. **reeky:** reeking; **chapless:** jawless.

A woman with a skeleton.
From Fabio Glissenti, *Discorsi morali contra il dispiacer del morire*
(1600).

Do thou but call my resolution wise 55
And with this knife I'll help it presently.
God joined my heart and Romeo's, thou our hands;
And ere this hand, by thee to Romeo's sealed,
Shall be the label to another deed,
Or my true heart with treacherous revolt 60
Turn to another, this shall slay them both.
Therefore, out of thy long-experienced time,
Give me some present counsel; or, behold,
'Twixt my extremes and me this bloody knife
Shall play the umpire, arbitrating that 65
Which the commission of thy years and art
Could to no issue of true honor bring.
Be not so long to speak. I long to die
If what thou speakst speak not of remedy.
  Friar. Hold, daughter. I do spy a kind of hope, 70
Which craves as desperate an execution
As that is desperate which we would prevent.
If, rather than to marry County Paris,
Thou hast the strength of will to slay thyself,
Then is it likely thou wilt undertake 75
A thing like death to chide away this shame,
That copest with death himself to scape from it;
And, if thou darest, I'll give thee remedy.
  Jul. O, bid me leap, rather than marry Paris,
From off the battlements of yonder tower, 80
Or walk in thievish ways, or bid me lurk
Where serpents are; chain me with roaring bears,
Or shut me nightly in a charnel house,
O'ercovered quite with dead men's rattling bones,
With reeky shanks and yellow chapless skulls; 85
Or bid me go into a new-made grave
And hide me with a dead man in his shroud—
Things that, to hear them told, have made me tremble—

97. **presently:** at once.

98. **humor:** liquid; see [II. i.] 33.

104. **supple government:** facility of movement.

107. **two-and-forty hours:** Shakespeare uses dramatic license here; the speedy movement of the play does not allow for a lapse of forty-two hours before Juliet awakens.

112. **uncovered:** i.e., with uncovered face.

116. **drift:** intention.

121. **inconstant toy:** whim of irresolution.

And I will do it without fear or doubt,
To live an unstained wife to my sweet love.　　90
　Friar. Hold, then. Go home, be merry, give consent
To marry Paris. Wednesday is tomorrow.
Tomorrow night look that thou lie alone;
Let not the nurse lie with thee in thy chamber.
Take thou this vial, being then in bed,　　95
And this distilled liquor drink thou off;
When presently through all thy veins shall run
A cold and drowsy humor; for no pulse
Shall keep his native progress, but surcease;
No warmth, no breath, shall testify thou livest;　　100
The roses in thy lips and cheeks shall fade
To paly ashes, thy eyes' windows fall
Like death when he shuts up the day of life;
Each part, deprived of supple government,
Shall, stiff and stark and cold, appear like death;　　105
And in this borrowed likeness of shrunk death
Thou shalt continue two-and-forty hours,
And then awake as from a pleasant sleep.
Now, when the bridegroom in the morning comes
To rouse thee from thy bed, there art thou dead.　　110
Then, as the manner of our country is,
In thy best robes uncovered on the bier
Thou shalt be borne to that same ancient vault
Where all the kindred of the Capulets lie.
In the mean time, against thou shalt awake,　　115
Shall Romeo by my letters know our drift;
And hither shall he come; and he and I
Will watch thy waking, and that very night
Shall Romeo bear thee hence to Mantua.
And this shall free thee from this present shame,　　120
If no inconstant toy nor womanish fear
Abate thy valor in the acting it.

[IV. ii.] As the Capulet household busily prepares for the wedding, Juliet returns to pretend docile submission to her parents' wishes. Her father is so delighted that he decides to have the wedding the next day and hurries off to inform Paris.

═══════════

14. **peevish:** silly; **harlotry:** good-for-nothing girl; Capulet doesn't mean to accuse Juliet literally of the behavior of a harlot.

Jul. Give me, give me! O, tell not me of fear!

Friar. Hold! Get you gone, be strong and prosperous
In this resolve. I'll send a friar with speed   125
To Mantua, with my letters to thy lord.

Jul. Love give me strength! and strength shall help
    afford.
Farewell, dear father.

                                  Exeunt.

[Scene II. Capulet's house.]

Enter *Father Capulet, Mother, Nurse,* and *Servingmen,*
two or three.

Cap. So many guests invite as here are writ.
                        [*Exit a Servingman.*]
Sirrah, go hire me twenty cunning cooks.

Serv. You shall have none ill, sir; for I'll try if they can
lick their fingers.

Cap. How canst thou try them so?   5

Serv. Marry, sir, 'tis an ill cook that cannot lick his
own fingers. Therefore he that cannot lick his fingers goes
not with me.

Cap. Go, begone.   *Exit Servingman.*
We shall be much unfurnished for this time.   10
What, is my daughter gone to Friar Laurence?

Nurse. Ay, forsooth.

Cap. Well, he may chance to do some good on her.
A peevish self-willed harlotry it is.

Enter *Juliet.*

Nurse. See where she comes from shrift with merry   15
    look.

21. **behests:** commands.
28. **becomed:** becoming; suitable.
30. **on't:** of it.
34. **bound:** indebted.
35. **closet:** private chamber.

Cap. How now, my headstrong? Where have you been
  gadding?

Jul. Where I have learnt me to repent the sin
Of disobedient opposition 20
To you and your behests, and am enjoined
By holy Laurence to fall prostrate here
To beg your pardon. Pardon, I beseech you!
Henceforward I am ever ruled by you.

Cap. Send for the County. Go tell him of this. 25
I'll have this knot knit up tomorrow morning.

Jul. I met the youthful lord at Laurence' cell
And gave him what becomed love I might,
Not stepping o'er the bounds of modesty.

Cap. Why, I am glad on't. This is well. Stand up. 30
This is as't should be. Let me see the County.
Ay, marry, go, I say, and fetch him hither.
Now, afore God, this reverend holy friar,
All our whole city is much bound to him.

Jul. Nurse, will you go with me into my closet 35
To help me sort such needful ornaments
As you think fit to furnish me tomorrow?

Mother. No, not till Thursday. There is time enough.

Cap. Go, nurse, go with her. We'll to church tomorrow.
                       Exeunt Juliet and Nurse.

Mother. We shall be short in our provision. 40
'Tis now near night.

Cap.   Tush, I will stir about,
And all things shall be well, I warrant thee, wife.
Go thou to Juliet, help to deck up her.
I'll not to bed tonight; let me alone. 45
I'll play the housewife for this once. What, ho!
They are all forth; well, I will walk myself
To County Paris, to prepare him up

[IV. iii.] Juliet dismisses her nurse for the night. After musing on the dreadful mishaps that may result from the drug, she finally summons her courage, drinks the vial, and falls into a trance.

●●●●●●●●●●●●●●●●●●●●●●●●●●●

3. **orisons:** prayers.
5. **cross:** irregular.
7. **culled:** chosen.
8. **behooveful:** needful; **state:** pomp.
16. **faint:** i.e., producing faintness in her.
20. **dismal:** dreadful.

Against tomorrow. My heart is wondrous light,
Since this same wayward girl is so reclaimed. 50

                              Exeunt.

[Scene III. Juliet's chamber.]

Enter *Juliet* and *Nurse*.

Jul. Ay, those attires are best; but, gentle nurse,
I pray thee leave me to myself tonight;
For I have need of many orisons
To move the heavens to smile upon my state,
Which, well thou knowest, is cross and full of sin. 5

Enter *Mother*.

Mother. What, are you busy, ho? Need you my help?
Jul. No, madam; we have culled such necessaries
As are behooveful for our state tomorrow.
So please you, let me now be left alone,
And let the nurse this night sit up with you; 10
For I am sure you have your hands full all
In this so sudden business.
Mother.   Good night.
Get thee to bed and rest, for thou hast need.
                Exeunt [*Mother and Nurse*].
Jul. Farewell! God knows when we shall meet again. 15
I have a faint cold fear thrills through my veins
That almost freezes up the heat of life.
I'll call them back again to comfort me.
Nurse!—What should she do here?
My dismal scene I needs must act alone.
Come, vial. 20

30. **tried:** shown by trial.

37. **like:** likely.

38. **conceit:** imagining.

43. **green in earth:** recently buried.

48. **mandrakes:** the roots of the plant *Mandragora officinarum,* which was popular for use in sleeping potions. The forked shape of the root was believed to resemble a human figure and when pulled up it was supposed to shriek and cause madness in the hearer.

MANDRAGORAS.

FOEMINA   MARIS

A mandrake.

From Rembert Dodoens, *Purgantium aliarumque* (1574).

What if this mixture do not work at all?
Shall I be married then tomorrow morning?
No, no! This shall forbid it. Lie thou there.

[*Lays down a dagger.*]

What if it be a poison which the friar   25
Subtly hath ministered to have me dead,
Lest in this marriage he should be dishonored
Because he married me before to Romeo?
I fear it is; and yet methinks it should not,
For he hath still been tried a holy man.   30
How if, when I am laid into the tomb,
I wake before the time that Romeo
Come to redeem me? There's a fearful point!
Shall I not then be stifled in the vault,
To whose foul mouth no healthsome air breathes in, 35
And there die strangled ere my Romeo comes?
Or, if I live, is it not very like
The horrible conceit of death and night,
Together with the terror of the place—
As in a vault, an ancient receptacle   40
Where for this many hundred years the bones
Of all my buried ancestors are packed;
Where bloody Tybalt, yet but green in earth,
Lies fest'ring in his shroud: where, as they say,
At some hours in the night spirits resort—   45
Alack, alack, is it not like that I,
So early waking—what with loathsome smells,
And shrieks like mandrakes torn out of the earth,
That living mortals, hearing them, run mad—
O, if I wake, shall I not be distraught,   50
Environed with all these hideous fears,
And madly play with my forefathers' joints,
And pluck the mangled Tybalt from his shroud,
And, in this rage, with some great kinsman's bone

58. **Stay:** hold, stop.

[IV. iv.] On the wedding morning the Capulet household is engaged in last-minute necessities for the wedding. The Nurse is sent to awaken Juliet.

Note: Some commentators, notably Harley Granville-Barker, feel that the dramatic effect here is heightened by having Juliet's bed separated from the audience merely by curtains, either the curtains of the bed itself or those of the inner stage. It would have been possible for the bed to have been set on the inner stage and for Juliet to have moved about toward the front stage area in order to be closer to the audience for her suspenseful preceding scene.

---

3. **pastry:** pantry.

9. **cot-quean:** housewife, literally; here used contemptuously for a man who interferes with woman's domestic work.

11. **For:** because of; **watching:** wakefulness.

14. **mouse-hunt:** literally, a name for the weasel, which stalks its prey at night; figuratively here, a woman-hunter.

As with a club dash out my desp'rate brains?   55
O, look! methinks I see my cousin's ghost
Seeking out Romeo, that did spit his body
Upon a rapier's point. Stay, Tybalt, stay!
Romeo, I come! this do I drink to thee.
    She [drinks and] falls upon her bed within the curtains.

[Scene IV. Capulet's house.]

Enter Lady of the House and Nurse.

Lady. Hold, take these keys and fetch more spices,
    nurse.
Nurse. They call for dates and quinces in the pastry.

Enter Old Capulet.

Cap. Come, stir, stir, stir! The second cock hath
    crowed,   5
The curfew bell hath rung, 'tis three o'clock.
Look to the baked meats, good Angelica;
Spare not for cost.
Nurse.   Go, you cot-quean, go,
Get you to bed! Faith, you'll be sick tomorrow   10
For this night's watching.
Cap. No, not a whit. What, I have watched ere now
All night for lesser cause, and ne'er been sick.
Lady. Ay, you have been a mouse-hunt in your time;
But I will watch you from such watching now.   15
                    Exeunt Lady and Nurse.
Cap. A jealous hood, a jealous hood!

25. **Mass:** by the Mass; **whoreson:** a term of good-natured familiarity meaning no more than "fellow."

26. **loggerhead:** blockhead. Capulet, in a good humor himself, enjoys the servant's humor.

[IV. v.] The Nurse discovers Juliet in a trance that appears to be death and the household breaks into lamentations. The merry wedding has turned to a dismal funeral.

Enter three or four [*Servants*], with spits and logs and
baskets.

                          Now, fellow,
What is there?
  1. Serv. Things for the cook, sir; but I know not what.
  Cap. Make haste, make haste. [*Exit Servant.*] Sirrah,   20
    fetch drier logs.
Call Peter; he will show thee where they are.
  2. Serv. I have a head, sir, that will find out logs
And never trouble Peter for the matter.
  Cap. Mass, and well said; a merry whoreson, ha!   25
Thou shalt be loggerhead. [*Exit Servant.*] Good faith, 'tis
    day.
The County will be here with music straight,
For so he said he would. (*Play music.*) I hear him near.
Nurse! Wife! What, ho! What, nurse, I say!   30

                Enter *Nurse*.

Go waken Juliet; go and trim her up.
I'll go and chat with Paris. Hie, make haste,
Make haste! The bridegroom he is come already:
Make haste, I say.

                            [*Exeunt.*]

              [Scene V. Juliet's chamber.]

                  [Enter *Nurse*.]

  Nurse. Mistress! what, mistress! Juliet! Fast, I warrant
her, she.
Why, lamb! why, lady! Fie, you slugabed!

7. **set up his rest:** determined.
29. **Out alas:** an exclamation of sorrow.

Why, love, I say! madam! sweetheart! Why, bride!
What, not a word? You take your pennyworths now!   5
Sleep for a week; for the next night, I warrant,
The County Paris hath set up his rest
That you shall rest but little. God forgive me!
Marry, and amen. How sound is she asleep!
I needs must wake her. Madam, madam, madam!   10
Ay, let the County take you in your bed!
He'll fright you up, i' faith. Will it not be?
                              [*Opens the curtains.*]
What, dressed and in your clothes and down again?
I must needs wake you. Lady! lady! lady!
Alas, alas! Help, help! my lady's dead!   15
O well-a-day that ever I was born!
Some aqua vitae, ho! My lord! my lady!

Enter *Mother*.

Mother. What noise is here?
Nurse.   O lamentable day!
Mother. What is the matter?   20
Nurse.   Look, look! O heavy day!
  Mother. O me, O me! My child, my only life!
Revive, look up, or I will die with thee!
Help, help! Call help.

Enter *Father*.

Father. For shame, bring Juliet forth; her lord is come.   25
Nurse. She's dead, deceased; she's dead! Alack the day!
  Mother. Alack the day, she's dead, she's dead, she's
    dead!
  Cap. Ha! let me see her. Out alas! she's cold,
Her blood is settled, and her joints are stiff;   30

46. **living:** income, material property.

47. **this morning:** i.e., the morning of his marriage to Juliet.

Life and these lips have long been separated.
Death lies on her like an untimely frost
Upon the sweetest flower of all the field.
   Nurse. O lamentable day!
   Mother.   O woeful time!   35
   Cap. Death, that hath ta'en her hence to make me
     wail,
Ties up my tongue and will not let me speak.

Enter *Friar* [*Laurence*] and the *County* [*Paris*], with
               Musicians.

   Friar. Come, is the bride ready to go to church?
   Cap. Ready to go, but never to return.   40
O son, the night before thy wedding day
Hath Death lain with thy wife. See, there she lies,
Flower as she was, deflowered by him.
Death is my son-in-law, Death is my heir;
My daughter he hath wedded. I will die   45
And leave him all. Life, living, all is Death's.
   Par. Have I thought long to see this morning's face,
And doth it give me such a sight as this?
   Mother. Accursed, unhappy, wretched, hateful day!
Most miserable hour that e'er time saw   50
In lasting labor of his pilgrimage!
But one, poor one, one poor and loving child,
But one thing to rejoice and solace in,
And cruel Death hath catched it from my sight!
   Nurse. O woe! O woeful, woeful, woeful day!   55
Most lamentable day, most woeful day
That ever ever I did yet behold!
O day! O day! O day! O hateful day!
Never was seen so black a day as this.
O woeful day! O woeful day!
                             60

67. **solemnity:** festivity; see I. [v.] 58.

71. **Confusion:** catastrophe; **cure:** Theobald's correction of " care" in the early texts.

89. **nature's tears are reason's merriment:** i.e., what human sentiment regrets common sense considers cause for rejoicing.

93. **cheer:** food.

94. **sullen:** mournful.

Par. Beguiled, divorced, wronged, spited, slain!
Most detestable Death, by thee beguiled,
By cruel cruel thee quite overthrown!
O love! O life! not life, but love in death!

    Cap. Despised, distressed, hated, martyred, killed! 65
Uncomfortable time, why camest thou now
To murder, murder our solemnity?
O child! O child! my soul, and not my child!
Dead art thou, dead! alack, my child is dead,
And with my child my joys are buried! 70

    Friar. Peace, ho, for shame! Confusion's cure lives not
In these confusions. Heaven and yourself
Had part in this fair maid! now heaven hath all,
And all the better is it for the maid.
Your part in her you could not keep from death, 75
But heaven keeps his part in eternal life.
The most you sought was her promotion,
For 'twas your heaven she should be advanced;
And weep ye now, seeing she is advanced
Above the clouds, as high as heaven itself? 80
O, in this love, you love your child so ill
That you run mad, seeing that she is well.
She's not well married that lives married long,
But she's best married that dies married young.
Dry up your tears and stick your rosemary 85
On this fair corse, and, as the custom is,
In all her best array bear her to church;
For though fond nature bids us all lament,
Yet nature's tears are reason's merriment.

    Cap. All things that we ordained festival 90
Turn from their office to black funeral—
Our instruments to melancholy bells,
Our wedding cheer to a sad burial feast;
Our solemn hymns to sullen dirges change;

100. ill: sin (committed by you).

104. case: situation, though the musician proceeds to pun on various meanings of the word.

Ent. after l. 105. The Second Quarto has "Enter Will Kemp," an indication that the part of Peter was played by Kemp, one of the most famous Elizabethan stage clowns.

106. "Heart's Ease": a popular song of the day.

111. dump: melancholy song or dance. Peter probably only hopes for a tune which will be less mournful than most dumps.

118. gleek: jeering speech.

118-19. give you the minstrel: i.e., as an insulting term I will call you "minstrel."

122. carry: bear, put up with; **crotchets:** fanciful notions, with a pun on the musical meaning "quarter notes."

Our bridal flowers serve for a buried corse;   95
And all things change them to the contrary.
    Friar. Sir, go you in; and, madam, go with him;
And go, Sir Paris. Every one prepare
To follow this fair corse unto her grave.
The heavens do lower upon you for some ill;   100
Move them no more by crossing their high will.

> *They all but the Nurse [and Musicians] go forth,
> casting rosemary on her and shutting the curtains.*

    1. Mus. Faith, we may put up our pipes and be gone.
    Nurse. Honest good fellows, ah, put up, put up!
For well you know this is a pitiful case.   [*Exit.*]
    1. Mus. Ay, by my troth, the case may be amended. 105

Enter *Peter*.

    Pet. Musicians, O, musicians, "Heart's Ease," Heart's
      Ease"]
O, an you will have me live, play "Heart's Ease."
    1. Mus. Why "Heart's Ease"?
    Pet. O, musicians, because my heart itself plays "My 110
heart is full of woe." O, play me some merry dump to
comfort me.
    1. Mus. Not a dump we! 'Tis no time to play now.
    Pet. You will not then?
    1. Mus. No.   115
    Pet. I will then give it you soundly.
    1. Mus. What will you give us?
    Pet. No money, on my faith, but the gleek. I will give
you the minstrel.
    1. Mus. Then will I give you the serving-creature.   120
    Pet. Then will I lay the serving-creature's dagger on
your pate. I will carry no crotchets. I'll re you, I'll fa you.
Do you note me?

125. **put out,** i.e., exhibit.

130-32. **When . . . sound:** an excerpt from Richard Edwardes' "In commendation of music." The poem is found in *The Paradise of Dainty Devices* (1576).

131. **dumps:** sorrows.

134. **Catling:** Peter is making up the last names of the musicians; a **catling** was a small lute string of catgut.

136. **Rebeck:** a stringed musical instrument; a sort of prototype of the violin.

139. **Soundpost:** a small post set under the bridge of a stringed instrument as a support and to transmit sound to the back.

141. **cry you mercy:** beg your pardon.

145. **redress:** aid, relief.

148. **stay:** i.e., stay for.

1. Mus. An you re us and fa us, you note us.

2. Mus. Pray you put up your dagger, and put out 125
your wit.

Pet. Then have at you with my wit! I will dry-beat
you with an iron wit, and put up my iron dagger. Answer
me like men.

"When griping grief the heart doth wound, 130
    And doleful dumps the mind oppress,
Then music with her silver sound"—

Why "silver sound"? Why "music with her silver sound"?
What say you, Simon Catling?

1. Mus. Marry, sir, because silver hath a sweet sound. 135

Pet. Pretty! What say you, Hugh Rebeck?

2. Mus. I say "silver sound" because musicians sound
for silver.

Pet. Pretty too! What say you, James Soundpost?

3. Mus. Faith, I know not what to say. 140

Pet. O, I cry you mercy! you are the singer. I will say
for you. It is "music with her silver sound" because musicians have no gold for sounding.

"Then music with her silver sound
    With speedy help doth lend redress." *Exit.* 145

1. Mus. What a pestilent knave is this same!

2. Mus. Hang him, Jack! Come, we'll in here, tarry for
the mourners, and stay dinner.

Exeunt.

THE TRAGEDY OF

ROMEO AND JULIET

ACT V

[V. i.] Balthasar, Romeo's servant, brings him word that Juliet is dead and buried in the Capulet vault. Romeo decides to join her in death and, buying poison from an apothecary, sets out for Verona.

━━━━━━━━━━━━━━━━━━━━

3. **bosom's lord:** i.e., heart.
7. **gives . . . leave:** allows.

[ACT V]

Enter *Romeo.*

Rom. If I may trust the flattering truth of sleep,
My dreams presage some joyful news at hand.
My bosom's lord sits lightly in his throne,
And all this day an unaccustomed spirit
Lifts me above the ground with cheerful thoughts.   5
I dreamt my lady came and found me dead
(Strange dream that gives a dead man leave to think!)
And breathed such life with kisses in my lips
That I revived and was an emperor.
Ah me! how sweet is love itself possessed,   10
When but love's shadows are so rich in joy!

Enter *Romeo's Man Balthasar,* booted.

News from Verona! How now, Balthasar?
Dost thou not bring me letters from the friar?
How doth my lady? Is my father well?
How fares my Juliet? That I ask again,   15
For nothing can be ill if she be well.
Bal. Then she is well, and nothing can be ill.
Her body sleeps in Capel's monument,
And her immortal part with angels lives.
I saw her laid low in her kindred's vault   20
And presently took post to tell it you.

23. **office:** duty.

41. **weeds:** clothing; **overwhelming:** i.e., over-hanging (because frowning in his anxiety).

42. **Culling:** sorting; see [IV. iii.] 7; **simples:** herbs.

47. **account:** showing.

49. **packthread:** wrapping twine; **cakes of roses:** small bales of rose petals, used in cosmetics and condiments.

53. **present:** immediate.

54. **caitiff:** miserable.

An apothecary's shop.
From Hartmann Schopper, *Panoplia* (1568).

O, pardon me for bringing these ill news,
Since you did leave it for my office, sir.

  Rom. Is it e'en so? Then I defy you, stars!
Thou knowst my lodging. Get me ink and paper   25
And hire posthorses. I will hence tonight.

  Bal. I do beseech you, sir, have patience.
Your looks are pale and wild and do import
Some misadventure.

  Rom.   Tush, thou art deceived.   30
Leave me and do the thing I bid thee do.
Hast thou no letters to me from the friar?

  Bal. No, my good lord.

  Rom.   No matter. Get thee gone
And hire those horses. I'll be with thee straight.   35

                       Exit [Balthasar].

Well, Juliet, I will lie with thee tonight.
Let's see for means. O mischief, thou art swift
To enter in the thoughts of desperate men!
I do remember an apothecary,
And hereabouts he dwells which late I noted   40
In tattered weeds, with overwhelming brows,
Culling of simples. Meager were his looks,
Sharp misery had worn him to the bones;
And in his needy shop a tortoise hung,
An alligator stuffed, and other skins   45
Of ill-shaped fishes; and about his shelves
A beggarly account of empty boxes,
Green earthen pots, bladders, and musty seeds,
Remnants of packthread, and old cakes of roses
Were thinly scattered, to make up a show.   50
Noting this penury, to myself I said,
"An if a man did need a poison now
Whose sale is present death in Mantua,
Here lives a caitiff wretch would sell it him."

62. **ducats:** gold coins.
63. **gear:** stuff; see [II. iv.] 99.
66. **trunk:** body.
69. **mortal:** deadly.
70. **utters:** distributes.

O, this same thought did but forerun my need,   55
And this same needy man must sell it me.
As I remember, this should be the house.
Being holiday, the beggar's shop is shut.
What, ho! apothecary!

Enter *Apothecary*.

Apoth.   Who calls so loud?   60
Rom. Come hither, man. I see that thou art poor.
Hold, there is forty ducats. Let me have
A dram of poison, such soon-speeding gear
As will disperse itself through all the veins
That the life-weary taker may fall dead,   65
And that the trunk may be discharged of breath
As violently as hasty powder fired
Doth hurry from the fatal cannon's womb.
Apoth. Such mortal drugs I have; but Mantua's law
Is death to any he that utters them.   70
Rom. Art thou so bare and full of wretchedness
And fearest to die? Famine is in thy cheeks,
Need and oppression starveth in thine eyes,
Contempt and beggary hangs upon thy back:
The world is not thy friend, nor the world's law;   75
The world affords no law to make thee rich;
Then be not poor, but break it and take this.
Apoth. My poverty but not my will consents.
Rom. I pay thy poverty and not thy will.
Apoth. Put this in any liquid thing you will   80
And drink it off, and if you had the strength
Of twenty men, it would dispatch you straight.
Rom. There is thy gold—worse poison to men's souls,
Doing more murder in this loathsome world,
Than these poor compounds that thou mayst not sell.   85

88. **cordial:** a substance which has a stimulating action on the heart.

▬▬▬▬▬▬▬▬▬▬▬▬▬▬▬▬▬▬▬▬▬

[V. ii.] Friar John reports to Friar Laurence that he has been unable to deliver his letter to Romeo. The letter had related the details of Juliet's forced wedding and the ruse designed to prevent it. Friar Laurence, much worried, hurries to the Capulet vault to be on hand when Juliet awakens.

▬▬▬▬▬▬▬▬▬▬▬▬▬

6. **associate:** company.

8. **searchers:** officials who investigated the causes of death in order to prevent the spread of contagious disease.

18. **nice:** trifling; see [III. i.] 157; **charge:** importance.

19. **dear:** an intensive indicating how very important the business was; see [III. iii.] 30.

I sell thee poison; thou hast sold me none.
Farewell. Buy food and get thyself in flesh.
Come, cordial and not poison, go with me
To Juliet's grave; for there must I use thee.

Exeunt.

[Scene II. *Verona.* Friar Laurence's cell.]

Enter *Friar John* to *Friar Laurence.*

John. Holy Franciscan friar, brother, ho!

Enter *Friar Laurence.*

Laur. This same should be the voice of Friar John.
Welcome from Mantua. What says Romeo?
Or, if his mind be writ, give me his letter.
John. Going to find a barefoot brother out,   5
One of our order to associate me,
Here in this city visiting the sick,
And finding him, the searchers of the town,
Suspecting that we both were in a house
Where the infectious pestilence did reign,   10
Sealed up the doors, and would not let us forth,
So that my speed to Mantua there was stayed.
Laur. Who bare my letter, then, to Romeo?
John. I could not send it—here it is again—
Nor get a messenger to bring it thee,   15
So fearful were they of infection.
Laur. Unhappy fortune! By my brotherhood,
The letter was not nice, but full of charge,
Of dear import; and the neglecting it
May do much danger. Friar John, go hence,   20

21. **crow:** crowbar.
26. **beshrew:** blame severely.
27. **accidents:** happenings.

━━━━━━━━━━━━━━━━━━━━

[V. iii.] Romeo finds Paris at the Capulet tomb and kills him when he will not leave. Friar Laurence arrives too late. Romeo has just drunk the fatal potion. When Juliet revives, the Friar tries to hurry her from the tomb but when she sees Romeo's body she refuses to leave and the Friar, frightened by the voices of the watch, departs. Juliet stabs herself with Romeo's dagger. Summoned by Paris' servant, the watch enters and finds the bodies. The Prince and the Capulet and Montague families arrive, and Friar Laurence tells the whole story of the young lovers. Chastened by the series of calamities, Capulet and Montague agree to end their senseless feud.

━━━━━━━━━━━━━━━━━━━━

14. **sweet water:** perfume.
15. **wanting:** lacking.

Get me an iron crow and bring it straight
Unto my cell.

   John.   Brother, I'll go and bring it thee.   *Exit.*
   Laur. Now must I to the monument alone.
Within this three hours will fair Juliet wake.   25
She will beshrew me much that Romeo
Hath had no notice of these accidents;
But I will write again to Mantua,
And keep her at my cell till Romeo come—
Poor living corse, closed in a dead man's tomb!   30

                                        Exit.

[Scene III. A churchyard with the Capulets' tomb.]

Enter *Paris* and his *Page* with flowers and [a torch].

   Par. Give me thy torch, boy. Hence, and stand aloof.
Yet put it out, for I would not be seen.
Under yond yew tree lay thee all along,
Holding thine ear close to the hollow ground.
So shall no foot upon the churchyard tread   5
(Being loose, unfirm, with digging up of graves)
But thou shalt hear it. Whistle then to me,
As signal that thou hearst something approach.
Give me those flowers. Do as I bid thee, go.
   Page. [*Aside*] I am almost afraid to stand alone   10
Here in the churchyard; yet I will adventure.
                             [*Withdraws.*]
   Par. Sweet flower, with flowers thy bridal bed I strew
                He strews the tomb with flowers.
(O woe! thy canopy is dust and stones)
Which with sweet water nightly I will dew;
Or, wanting that, with tears distilled by moans.   15

20. **cross:** hinder; **obsequies:** funeral rites.
S.D. after l. 21. **mattock:** a digging tool.
33. **jealous:** suspicious.

The obsequies that I for thee will keep
Nightly shall be to strew thy grave and weep.

Whistle Boy.

The boy gives warning something doth approach.
What cursed foot wanders this way tonight
To cross my obsequies and true love's rite?   20
What, with a torch? Muffle me, night, awhile.

[*Withdraws.*]

Enter *Romeo,* and *Balthasar* with a torch, a mattock, and
a crow of iron.

Rom. Give me that mattock and the wrenching iron.
Hold, take this letter. Early in the morning
See thou deliver it to my lord and father.
Give me the light. Upon thy life I charge thee,   25
Whate'er thou hearest or seest, stand all aloof
And do not interrupt me in my course.
Why I descend into this bed of death
Is partly to behold my lady's face,
But chiefly to take thence from her dead finger   30
A precious ring—a ring that I must use
In dear employment. Therefore hence, be gone.
But if thou, jealous, dost return to pry
In what I farther shall intend to do,
By heaven, I will tear thee joint by joint   35
And strew this hungry churchyard with thy limbs.
The time and my intents are savage-wild,
More fierce and more inexorable far
Than empty tigers or the roaring sea.

Bal. I will be gone, sir, and not trouble you.   40
Rom. So shalt thou show me friendship. Take thou that.
Live, and be prosperous; and farewell, good fellow.

Bal. [*Aside*] For all this same, I'll hide me hereabout.
His looks I fear, and his intents I doubt.   [*Withdraws.*]

45. **maw:** stomach.
48. **in despite:** with malice.
68. **conjuration:** entreaty.

T E R Z A
QVINTA GVARDIA STRETTA,
difenſiua, perfetta; nata da meza punta ſopra-
mano, offenſiua, da cui naſce un mezo
roueſcio tondo.

A dueling stance.
From Angelo Vizani, *Trattato dello schermo* (1588).

Rom. Thou detestable maw, thou womb of death,   45
Gorged with the dearest morsel of the earth,
Thus I enforce thy rotten jaws to open,
And in despite I'll cram thee with more food.
                              Romeo opens the tomb.

Par. This is that banisht haughty Montague
That murdered my love's cousin—with which grief   50
It is supposed the fair creature died—
And here is come to do some villainous shame
To the dead bodies. I will apprehend him.
Stop thy unhallowed toil, vile Montague!
Can vengeance be pursued further than death?   55
Condemnèd villain, I do apprehend thee.
Obey, and go with me; for thou must die.

Rom. I must indeed; and therefore came I hither.
Good gentle youth, tempt not a desp'rate man.
Fly hence and leave me. Think upon these gone;   60
Let them affright thee. I beseech thee, youth,
Put not another sin upon my head
By urging me to fury. O, be gone!
By heaven, I love thee better than myself,
For I come hither armed against myself.   65
Stay not, be gone. Live, and hereafter say
A madman's mercy bid thee run away.

Par. I do defy thy conjuration
And apprehend thee for a felon here.

Rom. Wilt thou provoke me? Then have at thee, boy!   70
                              They fight.

Page. O Lord, they fight! I will go call the watch.
                              [*Exit.*]

Par. O, I am slain! [*Falls.*] If thou be merciful,
Open the tomb, lay me with Juliet.   [*Dies.*]

Rom. In faith, I will. Let me peruse this face.
Mercutio's kinsman, noble County Paris!   75

83. **triumphant:** splendid.

84. **lantern:** a many-windowed tower atop a building such as a cathedral.

86. **feasting presence:** festive reception room for royal affairs of state.

87. **Death:** i.e., Paris' corpse.

What said my man when my betossed soul
Did not attend him as we rode? I think
He told me Paris should have married Juliet.
Said he not so? or did I dream it so?
Or am I mad, hearing him talk of Juliet,   80
To think it was so? O, give me thy hand,
One writ with me in sour misfortune's book!
I'll bury thee in a triumphant grave.
A grave? O, no, a lantern, slaughtered youth,
For here lies Juliet, and her beauty makes   85
This vault a feasting presence full of light.
Death, lie thou there, by a dead man interred.

     [Lays Paris in the tomb.]

How oft when men are at the point of death
Have they been merry! which their keepers call
A lightning before death O, how may I   90
Call this a lightning? O my love! my wife!
Death that hath sucked the honey of thy breath,
Hath had no power yet upon thy beauty.
Thou art not conquered. Beauty's ensign yet
Is crimson in thy lips and in thy cheeks,   95
And death's pale flag is not advanced there.
Tybalt, liest thou there in thy bloody sheet?
O, what more favor can I do to thee
Than with that hand that cut thy youth in twain
To sunder his that was thine enemy?   100
Forgive me, cousin! Ah, dear Juliet,
Why art thou yet so fair? Shall I believe
That unsubstantial Death is amorous,
And that the lean abhorred monster keeps
Thee here in dark to be his paramour?   105
For fear of that I still will stay with thee
And never from this palace of dim night
Depart again. Here, here will I remain

110. **set up my everlasting rest:** take my eternal rest, with a pun on the meaning from a card game known as "primero": to stake everything; see also [IV. v.] 7.

115. **dateless:** eternal; **engrossing:** monopolizing; a commercial term for buying in large quantities with intent to monopolize a commodity.

With worms that are thy chambermaids. O, here
Will I set up my everlasting rest   110
And shake the yoke of inauspicious stars
From this world-wearied flesh. Eyes, look your last!
Arms, take your last embrace! and, lips, O you
The doors of breath, seal with a righteous kiss
A dateless bargain to engrossing death!   115
Come, bitter conduct; come, unsavory guide!
Thou desperate pilot, now at once run on
The dashing rocks thy seasick weary bark!
Here's to my love! [*Drinks.*] O true apothecary!
Thy drugs are quick. Thus with a kiss I die.   *Falls.* 120

Enter *Friar* [*Laurence*], with lantern, crow, and spade.

  Friar. Saint Francis be my speed! how oft tonight
Have my old feet stumbled at graves! Who's there?
  Bal. Here's one, a friend, and one that knows you well.
  Friar. Bliss be upon you! Tell me, good my friend,
What torch is yond that vainly lends his light   125
To grubs and eyeless skulls? As I discern,
It burneth in the Capels' monument.
  Bal. It doth so, holy sir; and there's my master,
One that you love.
  Friar.   Who is it?   130
  Bal.   Romeo.
  Friar. How long hath he been there?
  Bal.   Full half an hour.
  Friar. Go with me to the vault.
  Bal.   I dare not, sir.   135
My master knows not but I am gone hence,
And fearfully did menace me with death
If I did stay to look on his intents.

140. **unthrifty:** unlucky.
153. **comfortable:** comforting.
163. **question:** argue.
167. **timeless:** untimely.
168. **churl:** niggard or miser.

Friar. Stay then; I'll go alone. Fear comes upon me.
O, much I fear some ill unthrifty thing.   140
Bal. As I did sleep under this yew tree here,
I dreamt my master and another fought,
And that my master slew him.
Friar.   Romeo!
    Stoops and looks on the blood and weapons.
Alack, alack, what blood is this which stains   145
The stony entrance of this sepulcher?
What mean these masterless and gory swords
To lie discolored by this place of peace?
               [Enters the tomb.]
Romeo! O, pale! Who else? What, Paris too?
And steeped in blood? Ah, what an unkind hour   150
Is guilty of this lamentable chance!
The lady stirs.
                    Juliet rises.
Jul. O comfortable friar! where is my lord?
I do remember well where I should be,
And there I am. Where is my Romeo?   155
Friar. I hear some noise. Lady, come from that nest
Of death, contagion, and unnatural sleep.
A greater power than we can contradict
Hath thwarted our intents. Come, come away.
Thy husband in thy bosom there lies dead;   160
And Paris too. Come, I'll dispose of thee
Among a sisterhood of holy nuns.
Stay not to question, for the watch is coming.
Come, go, good Juliet. I dare no longer stay.
Jul. Go, get thee hence, for I will not away.   165
                   Exit [Friar].
What's here? A cup, closed in my true love's hand?
Poison, I see, hath been his timeless end.
O churl! drunk all, and left no friendly drop

170. **Haply:** perhaps.

171. **restorative:** his kiss, if he were alive, would have that effect.

174. **happy:** opportune; see [III. v.] 116.

180. **attach:** arrest.

186. **woes:** woeful things; that is, the three bodies.

188. **circumstance:** a full explanation; see [II. v.] 37; **descry:** discern.

To help me after? I will kiss thy lips.
Haply some poison yet doth hang on them   170
To make me die with a restorative.   [*Kisses him.*]
Thy lips are warm!

    Chief Watch. [*Within*] Lead, boy. Which way?
    Jul. Yea, noise? Then I'll be brief. O happy dagger!
               [*Snatches Romeo's dagger.*]
This is thy sheath; there rest, and let me die.   175
              She stabs herself and falls.

Enter [*Paris'*] *Boy* and *Watch.*

    Boy. This is the place. There, where the torch doth
    burn.
    Chief Watch. The ground is bloody. Search about the
    churchyard.
Go, some of you; whoe'er you find attach.   180
               [*Exeunt some of the Watch.*]
Pitiful sight! here lies the County slain;
And Juliet bleeding, warm, and newly dead,
Who here hath lain this two days buried.
Go, tell the Prince; run to the Capulets;
Raise up the Montagues; some others search.   185
               [*Exeunt others of the Watch.*]
We see the ground whereon these woes do lie,
But the true ground of all these piteous woes
We cannot without circumstance descry.

Enter [*some of the Watch,*] with *Romeo's Man*
[*Balthasar*].

    2. Watch. Here's Romeo's man. We found him in the
    churchyard.   190

A man wearing a gown.
From Braun and Hogenberg's Map of London (1554-58).
(See S.D. after I. i. 75.)

197. **A great suspicion:** a very suspicious thing.
204. **startles:** starts up.

Chief Watch. Hold him in safety till the Prince come
hither.

Enter *Friar* [*Laurence*] and another *Watchman*.

3. Watch. Here is a friar that trembles, sighs, and
weeps.
We took this mattock and this spade from him   195
As he was coming from this churchyard side.
Chief Watch. A great suspicion! Stay the friar too.

Enter the *Prince* [and *Attendants*].

Prince. What misadventure is so early up,
That calls our person from our morning rest?

Enter *Capulet* and his *Wife* [with others].

Cap. What should it be, that they so shriek abroad?   200
Wife. The people in the street cry "Romeo,"
Some "Juliet," and some "Paris"; and all run,
With open outcry, toward our monument.
Prince. What fear is this which startles in our ears?
Chief Watch. Sovereign, here lies the County Paris   205
slain;
And Romeo dead; and Juliet, dead before,
Warm and new killed.
Prince. Search, seek, and know how this foul murder
comes.   210
Chief Watch. Here is a friar, and slaughtered Romeo's
man,
With instruments upon them fit to open
These dead men's tombs.
Cap. O heavens! O wife, look how our daughter bleeds! 215

216. **mista'en:** mistaken, missed its proper target; **his house:** i.e., the dagger's sheath.

220. **warns:** summons.

229. **Seal up the mouth of outrage:** that is, no more emotional outbursts.

234. **let mischance be slave to patience:** i.e., let patience rule your misfortunes instead of being overcome by them.

239. **impeach:** accuse; **purge:** clear.

This dagger hath mista'en, for, lo, his house
Is empty on the back of Montague,
And it missheathed in my daughter's bosom!
   Wife. O me! this sight of death is as a bell
That warns my old age to a sepulcher. 220

Enter *Montague* [and others].

   Prince. Come, Montague; for thou art early up
To see thy son and heir now early down.
   Mon. Alas, my liege, my wife is dead tonight!
Grief of my son's exile hath stopped her breath.
What further woe conspires against mine age? 225
   Prince. Look, and thou shalt see.
   Mon. O thou untaught! what manners is in this,
To press before thy father to a grave?
   Prince. Seal up the mouth of outrage for a while,
Till we can clear these ambiguities 230
And know their spring, their head, their true descent;
And then will I be general of your woes
And lead you even to death. Meantime forbear,
And let mischance be slave to patience.
Bring forth the parties of suspicion. 235
   Friar. I am the greatest, able to do least,
Yet most suspected, as the time and place
Doth make against me, of this direful murder;
And here I stand, both to impeach and purge
Myself condemned and myself excused. 240
   Prince. Then say at once what thou dost know in this.
   Friar. I will be brief, for my short date of breath
Is not so long as is a tedious tale.
Romeo, there dead, was husband to that Juliet;
And she, there dead, that Romeo's faithful wife. 245
I married them; and their stol'n marriage day

261. **borrowed:** temporary.
266. **prefixed hour:** time established in advance.
268. **closely:** secretly.
279. **privy:** that is, secretly cognizant of.

Was Tybalt's doomsday, whose untimely death
Banisht the new-made bridegroom from this city;
For whom, and not for Tybalt, Juliet pined.
You, to remove that siege of grief from her,　　　　250
Betrothed and would have married her perforce
To County Paris. Then comes she to me
And with wild looks bid me devise some mean
To rid her from this second marriage,
Or in my cell there would she kill herself.　　　　255
Then gave I her (so tutored by my art)
A sleeping potion; which so took effect
As I intended, for it wrought on her
The form of death. Meantime I writ to Romeo
That he should hither come as this dire night　　　　260
To help to take her from her borrowed grave,
Being the time the potion's force should cease.
But he which bore my letter, Friar John,
Was stayed by accident, and yesternight
Returned my letter back. Then all alone　　　　265
At the prefixed hour of her waking
Came I to take her from her kindred's vault;
Meaning to keep her closely at my cell
Till I conveniently could send to Romeo.
But when I came, some minute ere the time　　　　270
Of her awaking, here untimely lay
The noble Paris and true Romeo dead.
She wakes; and I entreated her come forth
And bear this work of heaven with patience;
But then a noise did scare me from the tomb,　　　　275
And she, too desperate, would not go with me,
But, as it seems, did violence on herself.
All this I know, and to the marriage
Her nurse is privy; and if aught in this
Miscarried by my fault, let my old life　　　　280

286. **in post:** posthaste, with all speed.
292. **raised:** roused, gave the alarm to.
299. **make good:** prove.
305. **scourge:** punishment.
306. **your joys:** i.e., your children.
310. **jointure:** dowry.

Be sacrificed, some hour before his time,
Unto the rigor of severest law.

   Prince. We still have known thee for a holy man.
Where's Romeo's man? What can he say in this?

   Bal. I brought my master news of Juliet's death;   285
And then in post he came from Mantua
To this same place, to this same monument.
This letter he early bid me give his father,
And threatened me with death, going in the vault,
If I departed not and left him there.   290

   Prince. Give me the letter. I will look on it.
Where is the County's page that raised the watch?
Sirrah, what made your master in this place?

   Boy. He came with flowers to strew his lady's grave;
And bid me stand aloof, and so I did.   295
Anon comes one with light to ope the tomb;
And by-and-by my master drew on him;
And then I ran away to call the watch.

   Prince. This letter doth make good the friar's words,
Their course of love, the tidings of her death;   300
And here he writes that he did buy a poison
Of a poor pothecary, and therewithal
Came to this vault to die and lie with Juliet.
Where be these enemies? Capulet, Montague,
See what a scourge is laid upon your hate,   305
That heaven finds means to kill your joys with love!
And I, for winking at your discords too,
Have lost a brace of kinsmen. All are punished.

   Cap. O brother Montague, give me thy hand.
This is my daughter's jointure, for no more   310
Can I demand.

   Mon.   But I can give thee more;
For I will raise her statue in pure gold,
That whiles Verona by that name is known,

315. at such rate be set: be so highly valued.

There shall no figure at such rate be set 315
As that of true and faithful Juliet.

  Cap. As rich shall Romeo's by his lady's lie—
Poor sacrifices of our enmity!

  Prince. A glooming peace this morning with it brings.
The sun for sorrow will not show his head. 320
Go hence, to have more talk of these sad things;
Some shall be pardoned, and some punished;
For never was a story of more woe
Than this of Juliet and her Romeo.

                        Exeunt omnes.

PREFERRED READINGS FROM

The First Quarto

First Quarto (spelling modernized)	Second Quarto
I. i. 123 the city's side	this City side
I. i. 180 create	created
I. i. 182 well-seeming	welseeing
I. i. 197 lovers'	louing
I. [ii.] 29 female	fennell
I. [ii.] 72 and	omitted
I. [iii.] 70, 71 honor	houre
I. [iii.] 103 it	omitted
I. [iv.] 7-8 Nor . . . entrance	omitted
I. [iv.] 46 like lamps	lights lights
I. [iv.] 62 Athwart	ouer
I. [iv.] 70 maid	man
I. [iv.] 76 O'er	On
I. [iv.] 85 dreams he	he dreams
I. [iv.] 94 elflocks	Elklocks
I. [iv.] 109 face	side
I. [v.] 15 have a bout	walke about
I. [v.] 47 Like	As
I. [v.] 100 ready stand	did readie stand
I. [v.] 141 there	here
[II. i.] 8 *Mer.*	*Ben.*

First Quarto (spelling modernized)	Second Quarto
[II. i.] 12 pronounce but "love" and "dove"	prouaunt, but loue and day
[II. i.] 15 trim	true
[II. i.] 40 open et cetera, thou	open, or thou
[II. ii.] 33 lazy-pacing	lazie puffing
[II. ii.] 43 nor . . . part	omitted
[II. ii.] 46 name	word
[II. ii.] 63 that . . . utterance	thy tongus vttering
[II. ii.] 65 saint	maide
[II. ii.] 74 let	stop
[II. ii.] 80 sight	eies
[II. ii.] 104 'havior	behauior
[II. ii.] 106 cunning	coying
[II. ii.] 112 swear	vow
[II. ii.] 174-75 my Romeo's name./ Romeo!	Romeo.
[II. ii.] 195 silk	silken
[II. iii.] 4 flecked	fleckled
[II. iii.] 5 fiery	burning
[II. iii.] 23 sometime's	sometime
[II. iii.] 89 She whom I love	her I loue
[II. iv.] 20 I can tell you	omitted
[II. iv.] 23 rests me	he rests
[II. iv.] 29-30 fantasticoes	phantacies
[II. iv.] 61 Well said	Sure wit
[II. iv.] 101 *Ben.*	*Mer.*
[II. iv.] 106 fairer of the two.	fairer face.

First Quarto (spelling modernized)	Second Quarto
[II. iv.] 142 Marry farewell	omitted
[II. iv.] 161 into	in
[II. iv.] 209 Peter . . . before	Before and apace.
[III. i.] 122 Alive	He gan
[III. i.] 124 And fire-eyed	And fier end
[III. i.] 169 agile	aged
[III. i.] 192 hate's	hearts
[III. i.] 196 I	It
[III. ii.] 59 swounded	sounded
[III. ii.] 69 dear-loved	dearest
[III. ii.] 75 *Nur.*	*Jul.*
[III. ii.] 76 *Jul.*	*Nur.*
[III. iii.] 54 Thou	Then
[III. iii.] 100 Well	omitted
[III. iii.] 123 Or	And
[III. iii.] 127 too that lives in thee	that in thy life lies
[III. iii.] 153 misbehaved	mishaued
[III. iii.] 154 poutst upon	puts vp
[III. iv.] 35 very very	very
[III. v.] 44 my lord, my love, my friend?	loue, Lord, ay husband, friend,
[III. v.] 56 below	so lowe
[III. v.] 186-89 Day . . . sleeping	Day, night, houre, tide, time, work, play/ Alone in companie
[III. v.] 191 princely	noble

First Quarto (spelling modernized)	Second Quarto
[III. v.] 192 trained	liand
[IV. i.] 7 talked	talke
[IV. i.] 47 cure	care
[IV. i.] 80 yonder	any
[IV. iv.] 26 faith	father
[IV. v.] 87 In all	And in
[IV. v.] 136, 139 Pretty	Prates
[V. i.] 15 How fares my Juliet	How doth my Lady Juliet
[V. i.] 24 defy	denie
[V. i.] 79 pay	pray
[V. iii.] 3 yew tree	young trees
[V. iii.] 4 thine	thy
[V. iii.] 68 conjuration	commiration
[V. iii.] 141 yew	yong
[V. iii.] 175 rest	rust

KEY TO

Famous Lines and Phrases

A pair of star-crossed lovers . . .
   [*Chorus*—Pro. I. 6]

. . . sad hours seem long.
   [*Romeo*—I. i. 164]

Alas that love, so gentle in his view,

Should be so tyrannous and rough in proof!
   [*Benvolio*—I. i. 172–73]

I will make thee think thy swan a crow.
   [*Benvolio*—I. ii. 92]

Queen Mab . . . She is the fairies' midwife . . .
   [*Mercutio*—I. iv. 57–99]

O, she doth teach the torches to burn bright!

It seems she hangs upon the cheek of night

Like a rich jewel in an Ethiop's ear . . .
   [*Romeo*—I. v. 45–54]

You kiss by the book.
   [*Juliet*—I. v. 116]

My only love, sprung from my only hate!

Too early seen unknown, and known too late!
   [*Juliet*—I. v. 147–48]

He jests at scars that never felt a wound.

But soft! What light through yonder window breaks?
   [*Romeo*—II. ii. 1–2]

O Romeo, Romeo! wherefore art thou Romeo?
   [*Juliet*—II. ii. 35]

That which we call a rose

By any other name would smell as sweet.
   [*Juliet*—II. ii. 45–6]

O, swear not by the moon, the inconstant moon,

That monthly changes in her circled orb,

Lest that thy love prove likewise variable.
   [*Juliet*—II. ii. 114–16]

Love goes toward love as schoolboys from their books;

But love from love, towards school with heavy looks.
   [*Romeo*—II. ii. 167–68]

How silver-sweet sound lovers' tongues by night,

Like softest music to attending ears!
   [*Romeo*—II. ii. 177–78]

Good night, good night! Parting is such sweet sorrow,

That I shall say good night till it be morrow.

[*Juliet*—II. ii. 200–1]

Thy head is as full of quarrels as an egg is full of meat . .

[*Mercutio*—III. i. 21–2]

A plague o' both your houses!

[*Mercutio*—III. i. 90]

. . . 'tis not so deep as a well, nor so wide as a church door; but 'tis enough, 'twill serve.

[*Mercutio*—III. i. 96–7]

Gallop apace, you fiery-footed steeds . . .

[*Juliet*—III. ii. 1–31]

Wilt thou be gone? It is not yet near day.

It was the nightingale and not the lark,

That pierced the fearful hollow of thine ear.

[*Juliet*—III. v. 1–3]

Night's candles are burnt out, and jocund day

Stands tiptoe on the misty mountain tops.

[*Romeo*—III. v. 9–10]

Thank me no thankings, nor proud me no prouds . . .

[*Capulet*—III. v. 157]

. . . past hope, past cure, past help!

[*Juliet*—IV. i. 47]

Not stepping o'er the bounds of modesty.

[*Juliet*—IV. ii. 29]

Death, that hath sucked the honey of thy breath,

Hath had no power yet upon thy beauty.

[*Romeo*—V. iii. 92–3]

. . . never was a story of more woe

Than this of Juliet and her Romeo.

[*Prince*—V. iii. 323–24]